The Road to Robert

Cover Photo © Stephen LaVere

ISBN-13: 978-0-634-00907-5
ISBN-10: 0-634-00907-9

HAL•LEONARD®
CORPORATION
7777 W. BLUEMOUND RD. P.O. BOX 13819 MILWAUKEE, WI 53213

Visit Hal Leonard Online at
www.halleonard.com

CONTENTS

Preface

I originally intended this to be the book to end all books about Robert Johnson. Instead, it became a book to begin all future considerations on him. Through my discographical work and technical findings, I offer new general statements for scholars and fans to work from. What's more, I feel I have reopened the examination of some neglected musicians and styles that merit further study.

My musical discussion of Johnson's blues will be in marked contrast to the lyric and folkloric treatments that have mostly prevailed in Johnson scholarship (especially since Marcus 1975 and Palmer 1981). While such literary presentations have had varying degrees of effect and usefulness, they misleadingly portray the blues process as consisting of words alone, without taking into account the specific pitches and rhythms to which the words are sung. If there was an oral tradition among bluesmen, it was concerned with the craft of making music. Among the best of musicians, including Johnson, the so-called oral tradition did not require any words to communicate. With their keen ears they could apprehend and play back what one another was performing. This higher level of "tradition" was in fact musical thievery, and one theme of my narrative describes the ways that Johnson protected his best techniques from being imitated.

For biographical details, I have consulted the published research of Stephen LaVere (1990), Gayle Dean Wardlow,[1] and Mack McCormick.[2] The other secondary accounts I cited (listed in the bibliography) greatly relied on the work of these three. Although my narrative is presented in chronological order, it is not so much a biography as it is an account of a musical odyssey that future Johnson biographers will need to consider.

The recorded performances of Johnson and his contemporaries were my primary sources, and from them I tried to discern the musical practices and changing trends that Johnson as a musician would have encountered. Whenever possible, I tried to find the records from which Johnson may have borrowed musical ideas for his own surviving performances. I also took into account recorded "melodic precedents"—that is—records made before 1936 (the year of Johnson's first sessions) that share the same melodic ideas. In some cases, it is doubtful that Johnson actually heard some of these discs. These melodic precedents should not be taken as specific sources of melodic origins, but as indicators of broad musical trends in the blues that Johnson may have noticed.

My dependence on recordings does not imply that Johnson was an armchair musician. Since several records from 1932 and 1933 were poorly distributed during their initial releases and are now very scarce, I believe that he heard several big city pianists like Leroy Carr, Roosevelt Sykes, Jabo Williams, and Peetie Wheatstraw live. In addition, the pianists he knew personally may have imitated those stars. Carr, Sykes, Williams, and Wheatstraw were never recorded "live" on location before World War II. Yet their commercial studio sides contain many vocal and instrumental practices that would have almost certainly been used regardless of the song or the performing setting. There were certain pianistic devices I had to consider in broad contextual relevance to Johnson, regardless of whether or not he knew the records on which those devices are preserved.

Beginning with the melodic precedent and contextual discs, I attempted to reconstruct his musical times. In my research I was fortunate to have the latest (1997) edition of Robert M.W. Dixon, John Godrich, and Howard Rye's *Blues and Gospel Records 1890-1943,* and the Document Records CD series of pre-World War II ("prewar") blues and sacred music. Without them I could not have stood on firm discographic ground, nor could I have written chapters four and five, which are crucial to my discussion of Johnson's music.

---

[1] Calt and Wardlow 1989, and reported by Obrecht 1990.
[2] reported by Guralnick 1982

Acknowledgments

I am most indebted to author Dave Rubin for the opportunity to present my historical research in book form. It was Dave who wondered in 1996 if Johnson used different tunings than what other writers and transcribers ascribed to him. When he first asked me what I thought about the possibility of alternate tunings, I replied immediately that if such tunings can be deduced from the Johnson recordings, and if there was some way of showing that they were an integral part of his musical practice and thinking, the findings would change many conceptual approaches to Johnson and pre-World War II Mississippi blues. During the years of research and writing, Dave and I kept in constant contact by phone, fax, and electronic mail. Together we plumbed the depths of pre-war blues, spurring each other to new questions and alternate ways of listening to the music. I am also thankful to Dave for introducing me to Jeff Schroedl and Jim Schustedt, who helped to develop the research and its eventual publication in *GuitarOne* articles and books. This narrative is a historical presentation of the research conducted by myself, Dave, and a team of Hal Leonard music transcribers. Companion Hal Leonard volumes that incorporate our work are: *Robert Johnson: The New Transcriptions; Robert Johnson: King of the Delta Blues;* and *Acoustic Country Blues Guitar: Delta Blues Before Robert Johnson.* During the research stage, Dave acted as a diplomatic liaison along with Hal Leonard vice-president John Cerullo to the Robert Johnson estate, administered by Stephen LaVere.

To illustrate some musical points, I had to transcribe in music notation several passages from blues records not previously transcribed for publication. Examples 2A, 2B, 2C, 4, 7B, 11A, 14, 15A, 18, 21, 23A, 24A, 24C, 25A, 25B, 28, 31A, 31B, 34, 39, and 40 were transcribed by me from records, and I am indebted to my Hal Leonard editors for neatening my notation, engraving, and obtaining permissions for use (publishers are cited in each example). Additional thanks to my editors for providing the harmonica diagram (Fig. 16).

While writing this book at the University of Mississippi Music Library and Blues Archive, I took several opportunities to discuss Robert Johnson with University colleagues and visiting researchers, including Peter Aschoff, Bonnie Krause, Burnis Morris, Warren Steel, and Thomas Freeland. Portions of chapter 4 were presented as papers at American Musicological Society Southern Chapter meetings, Arkansas State University Delta Studies symposia, and the 1998 Rock and Roll Hall of Fame conference on Robert Johnson. For encouragement and helpful advice at these events, I thank Dr. Jan Herlinger, Dr. Wallace McKenzie, Dr. William Clements, Dr. Ric Burns, Robert Santelli, and Stephen LaVere. Gayle Dean Wardlow and Douglas Allanbrook read early drafts of several chapters, and their individual remarks were given every consideration. Special thanks to Dr. Barry Lee Pearson and Scott Baretta, who provided me with the two record reviews in the *New Masses* newspaper.

Finally, I would like to thank my staff at the Music Library and Blues Archive during my tenure there (1993–2001), including Laura Sullivan and Lynda McNeill Aldana, for their assistance and patience. I am also grateful to my University of Mississippi supervisors Nancy Fuller and Diane Graves for recognizing this research as a part of my professional duties.

CHAPTER ONE

The Sounds of the Delta

The Mississippi Delta is outlined by the Mississippi River on the west and by the Yazoo River on the east, with Memphis as its north point. During its modern history, the almond-shaped floodplain has been developed with waterways, railroads, and highways. No less indelible are the musical paths criss-crossing the Delta's timelines. Standing at one of these intersections is Robert Johnson, whose recorded performances are so dazzling as to obscure his years of progress and practice. To regard him only at his crossroads would be to pin him at the fleeting moments (scarcely two hours of recorded music) of his 1936-1937 recording sessions. The route that Johnson took may still be traced, and along it is a series of audible monuments in the fantastic soundscape of the Delta that lends perspective to his musical progress.

Exploitation of the Delta Begins

After claiming the Mississippi Delta as their domain, the earliest planters cautiously guarded it from all usurpers. In the 1840s, these white men envisioned the clearance of its thick jungles for agricultural exploitation. If a hundred acres could be cleared (despite the malaria or dysentery), dark rich land with deep and well inexhaustible topsoil would be available. Yet with the combination of heat, humidity, and mosquitoes, the odds of clearing much swampland were strongly against the landowners. Had they carved out their planting niches with their own hands, they would have justly deserved their heroic statures. But their goals were achieved on the labors of black slaves, who numbered up to a hundred strong on some farms. These men and women were put to work harder and longer than most slaves in other Southern states, and under more frightful conditions.[3] Many of the developed fields were intended for cotton instead of food and other sources of subsistence. In this way, the fateful pattern of the Delta as a commercial enterprise—and not as a communal setting—was begun.

By 1860, about ten percent of the Delta had been cleared.[4] The Civil War (1861-1865) and the ensuing emancipation of slaves in the southern states, however, temporarily halted this work. While taking military control of the Mississippi River from Memphis to Vicksburg during the War, the Union Navy had to contend with the Delta and its climate. Controlling the river's floods became a postwar goal of the Army Corps of Engineers, led by Andrew Humphreys. Throughout the 1870s and 1880s, Humphreys clashed with civilian engineers James Eads and Charles Ellet over whether fortified levees, reservoirs, or cutoffs were viable means of control. Eventually, the Mississippi River Commission chose to contain the river with levees only.[5] Accordingly, Mississippi levee boards constructed artificial embankments to prevent the river from spilling into the Delta. The swamps were then cleared at a faster rate than previously possible; thirty percent of the Delta would be converted to farmland by 1900.[6]

Train Sounds and Work Songs

Up through the Civil War, boats were the primary means of transport in the Delta. But after the levees were built, railroads came to define the routes of travel. Most prominent were the Illinois Central Railroad and the Southern Railroad, each acquiring over 700,000 acres of Delta land in 1881 as parts of business deals with the river commission.[7] In 1892, Illinois Central took over the Louisville, New Orleans, and Texas (LNO&T) Railway, linking Memphis with New Orleans, and renamed it the Yazoo and Mississippi Valley Railroad (although it was popularly known as "the Yellow Dog"). A later addition to the Illinois Central network in Mississippi was the Gulf and Ship Island Railroad, running from Jackson to Gulfport. The completion of the railroads enabled Delta planters to conduct their business on an industrial basis. Cotton magnates like LeRoy Percy and Will Dockery built large plantations with hundreds, if not thousands, of farmhands.

[3] Cobb, 7-28
[4] Cobb, 43
[5] Barry 1997, 89-92
[6] Cobb, 100
[7] Barry, 101

To pace themselves through the long and fatiguing workdays, laborers sang work hollers and listened for railroad trains. Long customary among blacks to devise chants for particular tasks, the men clearing the Delta sang melodies whose rhythms regulated the timing of their ax-falls. Son House's "My Black Mama" may well have begun as an ax-song (see Fig. 1). The rests in the vocal line would literally be where the ax would fall. According to the given task at hand, each line of such a chant would be repeated once or twice with no melodic changes. Later, we'll see how House adapted work chants into a 12-bar blues.

Fig. 1 – Son House, "My Black Mama, Part 1"

To figure what time of day it was without the use of clocks, laborers learned to listen for individual trains chugging on their appointed rounds. The words, tones, and rhythms in early recorded Delta blues are suffused with train sounds. Figs. 2A and 2B as played by Bukka White and Charlie Patton, respectively, suggest the train's machinery in cyclic motion over the rails. White was especially adept in imitating railroad crossing bells on his guitar (Fig. 2C). Robert Johnson, on his 1936 record "Rambling on My Mind," illustrated his lyric "Runnin' down to the station, catch that old first mail train I see" by evoking on his guitar the whistle of a train departing from a station (Fig. 2D).

Fig. 2A – Bukka White, "New Frisco Train"
(That Frisco Train)

Fig. 2B – Charlie Patton, "Moon Going Down"

Fig. 2C – Bukka White, "New Frisco Train"
(That Frisco Train)

Fig. 2D – Robert Johnson, "Ramblin' on My Mind"

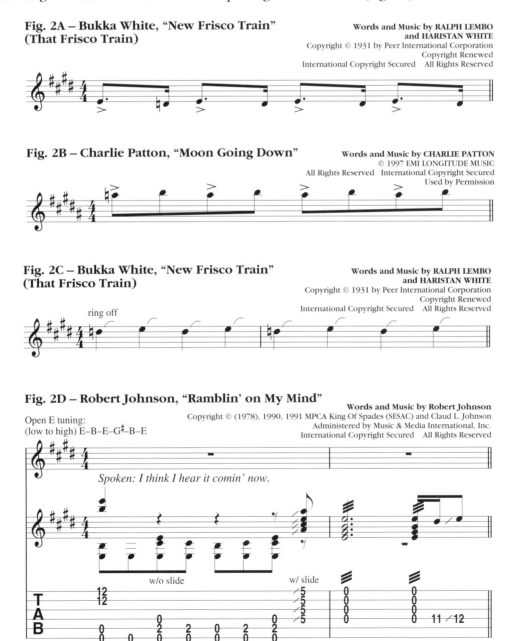

Sharecropping and Its Politics

Between the Civil War and World War II, sharecropping was the most common working arrangement between the Delta landowner and his tenant farmers. For one growing season with land and tools provided by the owner, the farmer would agree to give one-half of his resulting crop in return.[8] Sharecropping was introduced around 1868 when planters were lacking financial credit, labor, and capital. Blacks saw this arrangement as a step towards acquiring their own land.[9] In practice, though, the risks of cotton farming, including storms, droughts, and pests, were transferred to the tenants, and the value of a good crop varied from year to year due to the fluctuating cotton market. Although a few sharecroppers did earn enough money to start their own cotton farms, most of the others lived in poverty while toiling in vain for a profitable crop.

Cotton field, north of Morgan City, MS

Despite these risks, blacks from east and south Mississippi flocked to the newly cleared Delta plantations in the 1880s. However, the black population swelled so high in the Delta that the 1890 Mississippi constitutional convention drew "shoestring" voting districts to favor white candidates for public office. Such "reapportionment" was part of the regional move to "disenfranchise" blacks of their voting power.[10] Adding to such legislative woes was the 1896 U.S. Supreme Court decision in the case of Plessy vs. Ferguson, which lent sanction to public facilities (such as railroad cars and water fountains) for blacks "separate but equal" from those for whites. In Mississippi and other southern states, this resulted in separate but inferior facilities for blacks and other non-whites.

As the Delta continued to be cleared, the amount of farm work to be done began to outgrow the supply of sharecroppers to do it. Landowners began zealously guarding their more productive tenants from better terms from rival planters, enacting a new kind of economic slavery. To ease the strain of arduous fieldwork and oppressive new laws, many blacks sought new modes of creative expression in church and among friends to strengthen their spirits.

Black Sacred and Sanctified Music

Throughout the nineteenth century, blacks converting to Christian faiths usually became Baptists or Methodists.[11] Northern missionaries promoting literacy among the newly-freed blacks reinforced the social function of organized religion in black lives across the post-Civil War South. The founding of black colleges and universities such as Fisk University, Morehouse College, and in the Delta, Alcorn University (now Alcorn State University), extended the literacy mission into higher education.

Fisk University took initiative in the 1870s in notating black music (much of it remembered from slavery times) and promoting it through its Jubilee Singers tours and its widely distributed publications of sacred music. The Singers performed in restrained tempi and in close harmonies, with the sopranos and tenors rarely straying from more than an octave of each other except for dramatic passages. A 1915 arrangement of "I'm Going to Do All I Can" by John Wesley Work for the Singers (Fig. 3) neatly demonstrates the Jubilee style. The piece is in eight measures (although it could be transcribed in sixteen measures with doubled note values), and it proceeds in four phrases of two measures each. Most of the nineteenth century black religious repertory preserved in musical notation through the Fisk Singers and others (especially the 1867 publication *Slave Songs of the United States*) are eight measures or sixteen measures in length; some of it is eight+eight verse and refrain compounds, like "Go Down, Moses." The "Andante" tempo, the homophonic style of singing one chord per syllable, and the a cappella setting are especially typical of Jubilee arrangements. From 1870 through the 1930s, the Fisk Singers had many imitators, including commercial recording groups from black Mississippi college campuses like Rust College, Holly Springs, and Utica Institute, Utica.

---

[8] Cobb, 99
[9] Cobb, 55
[10] Cobb, 87-90
[11] Klatzko, 1966, 4

Fig. 3 – "I'm Going to Do All I Can"

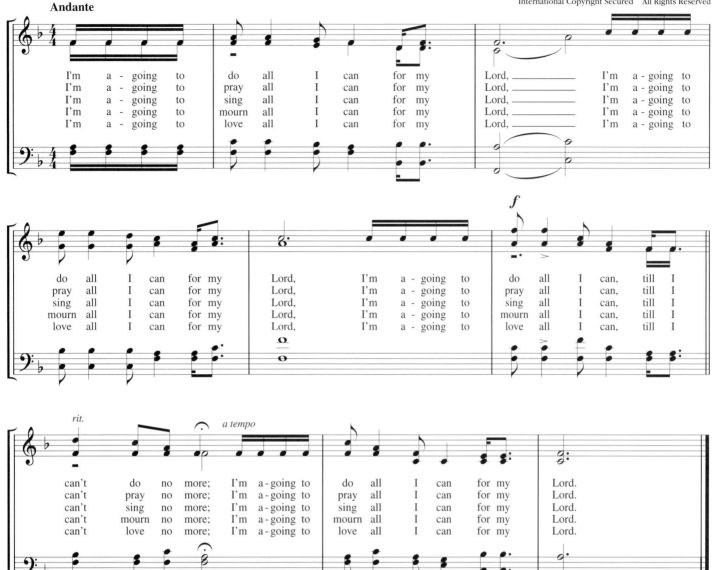

Despite the presence of Protestant religious faiths, many blacks who came to the Delta retained many of the old African dances and religious customs. With full exercise of their religious freedom (in contrast to their token political rights after the 1890 reapportionment), black Mississippians sought and developed new Christian faiths in which they could incorporate the African practices they remembered. The most notable of the new denominations was the Church of God in Christ (COGIC), also known as Holiness and Pentecostal. Although the plans for COGIC were drawn up in Memphis in 1895, the first congregation met the following year in Lexington, MS, just east of the Delta.[12] Religious ecstasy was a core element in COGIC meetings, and one means of achieving it was through "sanctified" music. Although using some of the same repertory as jubilee-style singers, sanctified singers used intervals of diminished fourths in their harmonies, the upper tones of which would be pushed by sopranos in harsh, raucous manners. Also, sanctified groups included instrumentalists—usually guitarists, banjo players, and percussionists—who would "open" the harmonic arrangement beyond the octave. The whole ensemble performed not homophonically, but bi-rhythmically or even polyrhythmically, and at faster tempi than the unaccompanied jubilee singers. The McIntorsh and Edwards recording of "Take a Stand," whose opening measures are given in Fig. 4, has three distinct rhythms: the unaccented vocal melody, the heavy quarter note beats in guitar 1, and the upbeats in the handclaps and guitar 2. In this way, the African practice of polyrhythm was retained and exercised.[13] The combination of these rhythmic layers by the earliest sanctified groups on records (1928-1930, many with Bessie Johnson, the quintessential sanctified lead singer) can easily transport the listener into ecstatic fervor.

---

[12] Klatzko, 1966, 3-4

[13] For a full presentation of African polyrhythms, see Arom 1991.

Melodic and Harmonic, Linear and Vertical

The jubilee and sanctified styles demonstrate separate kinds of musical processes. The sanctified style is a polyrhythmic and polyphonic type where the individual parts of the accompaniment are successively layered to the melody. In Fig. 4, the melody would be ably sung by lead singer Bessie Johnson alone, with Gtr. 1 stressing the individual beats to guide the tapping feet. The remaining performers fit where they can: the Elder singing an augmented fourth below Bessie Johnson; the clappers on the second and fourth beats, which is akin to the "Juba" dance rhythm long traditional among African Americans; and Gtr. 2 in quarter notes an octave below Gtr. 1. Each performer has an independent musical part to play or sing, but the only indispensable ones would be Bessie Johnson and Gtr. 1. The omission of any of the other performers will not affect the basic melodic presentation, although the total sound would be considerably lessened.

This independent polyrhythmic and polyphonic manner of performance I will call *linear,* as the separated melodies take on the appearance of horizontal lines when transcribed and notated on music paper. Usually the word "line" assumes the medium of space. Our musical use of "line" assumes the medium of time. Music notation translates the medium of time into that of space. For illustrations in this book, I will use examples of transcribed music. But in my discussion I will treat, as best as possible, melodies as distinctive and audible occurrences in time, without the immediate spatial properties of drawn lines.

On the other hand, the jubilee style depends on homophonic chords. One chord is given per syllable, and the component tones move and shift from one chord to the next in close accordance to the rhythms of each phrase. The top tone of each chord declaims the melody, and the bottom tone provides the solid tonal foundation. The middle tones fill out the rest of the triadic chord formation. Although the four singing parts are melodically independent of each other, they are bonded together to the overall tonality and the chosen harmonic progression. The arrangement is therefore not additive, but rather it is conceived, planned, and composed by one musician before the performance.

This harmonic homophonic style I will term *vertical*, in part acknowledging the visual appearance of chords in staff notation, but also in large part to the hierarchical manner we listen when tones in varying registers are sung or played. To be sure, "vertical" homophonic chords played sharply seem like lines, but when they are sustained they seem more like sound-blocks. To distinguish performed chords from one another, the element of rhythm in its melodic or harmonic forms will be important.

The musical concepts of melody and harmony, and the predominance of one over another towards a "linear" or "vertical" presentation (or rather, polyphonic or homophonic), loom large over the history of music in general. The particular manners that "linear" and "vertical" are heard in black music will be important towards understanding the musical transitions that occurred in the 1930s, as well as Robert Johnson's contributions to the overall stylistic change in Delta blues.

The Blues (8-, 16-, and 12-bar)

The turmoil of living and working in the 1890s Delta affected all blacks, regardless of faith. As vehicles of secular expression, the blues and its various structural forms were developed. The earliest printed appearances of several eight-measure and sixteen-measure blues melodies and chord progressions may be found in mid and late nineteenth century black sacred music collections. "I'm Gonna Do All I Can," for example, shares its melody with "You Gonna Need Somebody When You Gone to Die," "You Gonna Need Somebody on Your Bond," "See That My Grave Is Kept Clean," "There's a Man Going 'Round Taking Names," "Red River Blues," and, as will be seen later, Robert Johnson's "Last Fair Deal Gone Down."

The 12-bar blues, however, appears to be a combination of British dance forms, nineteenth century American popular music, and African-American melodic inflections.[14] Twelve-measure forms of three four-measure phrases are very unusual in nineteenth century music. Notable, though, are various British square dances that require twelve measure (four+four+four) musical structures.[15] It is likely that British emigrants brought such dances to the U.S., and that their descendants continued them as they founded farms and plantations across the South.[16] Meanwhile, in the mid nineteenth century, American popular music began making more frequent use of the subdominant (IV) chord to start new phrases between tonic openings and dominant phrases. This occurred in the 1830s "Zip Coon" (also sung as "Turkey in the Straw"), Stephen Foster's 1850 "Camptown Races," and "John Brown's Body" (later sung to the words "Battle Hymn of the Republic").[17] It was reported that "Frankie and Albert" was sung by Union troops at Vicksburg,[18] and if it was in the form that is common today, this may be the earliest known twelve-measure, I–IV–V song heard in the Delta.

Some Nuts and Bolts of the Blues

Some basic technical terms for certain blues music features will be used throughout this narrative. The words themselves may not be exactly the same as those used by Delta bluesmen in the 1930s, but they should signify the same musical "nuts-and-bolts" components they used to improvise their blues.

The *blues chorus* is the basic unit of the blues; it is repeated until the performer stops, whether he has sung all his lyrics, the dancers are tired, or the recording take is over. The chorus is typically in the forms of eight measures, twelve measures, and sixteen measures—each consisting of four-measure phrases. However, the eight-measure form may be either of two kinds: as a version of the sixteen-measure form renotated in shorter note values in four two-measure phrases, or as a descendant of the two-phrase spiritual.

The *12-measure* or *12-bar blues* is the most common chorus form used by Robert Johnson. The usual arrangement is of three four-measure phrases with four beats to a measure. Also, a typical *lyric scheme* for the 12-bar blues will be AAB—that is, one lyric will be sung during the first four-measure phrase, then repeated verbatim during the second phrase, and finally a rhyming lyric for the concluding phrase. The standard *harmonic* or *chord progression* for the 12-bar form is I–IV–V. The first phrase

---

[14] Much of the following is discussed in full in Rubin and Komara 1999.
[15] Sharp 1927
[16] Sharp 1917
[17] all reprinted in Jackson 1976
[18] Belden 1940, 330-333

is set in the tonic (I) chord; the second begins in the subdominant (IV) chord for two measures, then returns to I; and the third phrase starts in the dominant (V) chord for two measures, with the remaining two measures being the *chorus turnaround*. The turnaround is basically set in I, but often is executed with various deployments of the I and V chords.

Each four-measure phrase will usually have two parts, the *vocal lyric,* and the *instrumental fill.* The vocal lyric will be sung during the first two measures and the first beat of the third measure (that is, the first nine beats of the sixteen-beat phrase). The instrumental fill will take up the rest of the third measure and continue into the fourth (the remaining seven beats). Fills will generally be of two kinds: *licks* and *ornaments.* Licks will be of two measures, executed in the medium and high ranges of the accompanying instruments. Ornaments will be of short duration—usually one or two beats. Johnson will play ornaments during his lyric phrases as well as during his fills. The coordination of lyric phrases and instrumental fills results in what some writers have termed "the call and response pattern," as akin to the pattern of communication between a preacher and his congregation during religious services.

Crossing the Dog

The blues as an African-American tradition began when black musicians and composers across the South fit melodies with African inflections to the twelve-measure form and added lyrics intended for black audiences. The earliest Delta blues appear to have been improvised from the regional work chants, religious songs, and dances with the instruments at hand. W.C. Handy's account of hearing a slide guitarist at a Tutwiler train station in 1903 is a good example. According to Handy's description, the musician sang "Going to where the Southern crosses the Dog," referring to Morehead, where the Southern Railroad and the "Yellow Dog" (Yazoo and Mississippi Valley) Railroad meet. This lyric was repeated twice, and it was accompanied with a slide guitar technique (performed with a pocketknife) to a modality that fascinated Handy.[19]

Even then, the guitar was the prevailing musical instrument for accompanying Delta blues. How it was introduced in the Delta is fairly uncertain, although Gayle Wardlow's suggestion to the author that it was brought by Mexican laborers is plausible in view of the Delta's development. The offering of guitars for sale in Sears catalogs at the turn-of-the-century is another possibility. Pianos were less common in the Delta than elsewhere in Mississippi, possibly due to the fact that the small clusters of sharecroppers living near their individual fields could not afford them. Guitars, on the other hand, were portable, light, and cheap. Stella guitars, the make most often purchased by early Delta bluesmen, usually cost ten dollars each and, despite their cheap construction, had a good resonant sound. However, flat top acoustic guitars were barely audible in a juke full of dancers on a wooden floor; resonator guitars in the 1920s helped bluesmen to be heard a little better, but the innovations in electric guitar amplification would not come until the late 1930s. Also, all guitars through 1932 had only twelve frets. The introduction of fourteen-fret models would increase the individual string ranges from an octave to an octave plus a whole tone. This addition would allow the guitarist to place a capo on the first or second fret and still retain an octave range, without risking strain on the strings by retuning.

The guitarist that Handy heard in 1903 was probably among the first generation of Delta bluesmen who broadly forged the blues forms while the Delta was being cleared and the railroads were being built. The next generation, including Charlie Patton and Tommy Johnson, codified distinctive themes such as "Pony Blues" and "Maggie Campbell Blues," and then later in the 1920s made the first records of Delta blues. Although Robert Johnson and his fellow members of the third generation each had their particular teachers, they all looked to one hero from the previous era: Charlie Patton.

---

[19] Handy 1941, 74

Charlie Patton

Bukka White: "I always wanted to be like old Charlie Patton, long time ago when I was a kid out here, and play them numbers about 'Hitch up my buggy [sic] and saddle up my black mare.'"[20]

Howlin' Wolf: "I didn't start to fooling with guitar until about 1928, however, and I started on account on the plantation—Young and Mara's plantation, where our family was living—there was a guy at that time playing the guitar. He was called Charlie Patton. It was he who got me interested."[21]

Charlie Patton was born in 1891 in Edwards, MS and came with his family to the Dockery plantation in the Delta in the early 1900s. From around 1908, he made his living playing blues and other dance music at picnics, jukes, and house parties. A small man of slight build with a deep, hoarse voice, he nonetheless stood as a giant among his blues peers.[22] He was best known for dance numbers like "Pony Blues," "Banty Rooster Blues," and "Screamin' and Hollerin' the Blues." He was also a versatile sacred music performer, capable of singing hymns in the slow, controlled Protestant manner or with sanctified abandon. Although based in the Dockery vicinity during the 1910s and 1920s, he traveled widely, his music and showmanship in great demand everywhere in the Delta. Before long he became famous among the poor and oppressed blacks for leading a life of his own outside the cotton fields.

Patton was a "linear" type of performer—one who would add a treble layer of knife-fretted slide licks and an assortment of percussive guitar taps, body pats, and foottaps. His 1929 recording of "You Gone Need Somebody When You Come to Die" could not be more different than the Fisk jubilee arrangement of "I'm Gonna Do All I Can," although both share the same melody and both have a religious intent. The basic chords are strummed on open guitar strings, while simple two-note knife slide licks are executed on the top string. Although consonant with one another, the basic strum and the slide tones are an octave or more apart, and are not interdependent or connected with homophonic chords. Sometimes, each lyric phrase is one or two beats shorter or longer than they need or should be. In "linear" blues and sacred playing, the melody and its words get high priority for full expression, and formal considerations such as harmonic structure have to give way. Patton's blues and sacred records have a rhythmic bump-and-tumble quality due to his "linear" improvising and his seemingly irregular phrasing, but those of his imitators can sound downright ragged.

When Patton moved to Lula in 1930 and began playing regularly there, he became an important model to an aspiring bluesman from nearby Robinsonville: Robert Johnson.

---

[20] Samuel Charters, 1967, 34
[21] Pete Welding, 1967, 20
[22] For a biography, see Calt and Wardlow 1988.

CHAPTER TWO

"Let Him Learn!": The Apprenticeship of Robert Johnson

The Early Years of Robert Johnson

Robert Johnson was born on May 8, 1911, in Hazlehurst, Mississippi, forty miles southeast of the Delta.[23] The seat of Copiah County, it was named after George H. Hazlehurst, chief engineer of the Illinois Central Railroad, indicating the railroad's looming presence.[24]

If what Johnson's biographers[25] have reported is true, the circumstances surrounding his birth and upbringing are every bit as colorful as those about his death. His mother was Julia Major Dodds, whose landowning carpenter husband had fled Hazlehurst with his mistress in 1907 or 1909 under a threat of mob violence. Left behind, Mrs. Dodds had an affair with a man named Noah Johnson, and by him she gave birth to Robert. Before the end of 1911, though, she took her infant son and a daughter from Hazlehurst and, after a few years elsewhere in the Delta, placed them in the care of her estranged husband in Memphis, now living under the alias of Charles Spencer. She then married in 1916 a sharecropper near Robinsonville, MS, named Willie "Dusty" Willis (some writers have the stepfather's surname as "Saunders"[26]) and two years later received her son Robert back into her household.

These real and assumed names of Johnson's parents and guardians must have been as myriad and perplexing to him then as they are to us now. Yet, apparently when he learned the name of his biological father, he took the surname of Johnson. Biographers have had to be patient with their informants' attempts to remember one and the same person by several different names. He was known variously as Robert, R.L., and Bob, with a surname of Johnson, Dodds, Spencer, Dusty, Saunders, and Saxton, among others. It is fortunate that Johnson chose to have his records released under his true name, and that the state certificate of his death listed the Johnson name instead of the aliases he used while traveling. Otherwise, many of the known facts of his life would have been buried under a confusion of names.

While growing up around Robinsonville in the mid-1920s, Johnson began playing music on a harmonica. Although biographer Peter Guralnick[27] relates a story that Johnson, while living with the Spencers in the late 1910s, learned some rudimentary guitar from his half brother Charles Leroy Dodds, such playing may have been limited to plinking spare melodies on single strings. In any event, there seems to be no trace of songs from that particular era on Johnson's records. The earliest memories of him by those outside his family, including R.L. Windum,[28] Willie and Elizabeth Glynn Moore, and Evie House[29] are as a harmonica player on a cheap instrument.

Beginning the Guitar

Around 1928 or 1929, Johnson began playing guitar, although perhaps not too well. An idea of what he sounded like then can be gleaned from Elizabeth Glynn Moore, who related to Gayle Wardlow in 1969 his early lesson with her first husband, Harvey "Hard Rock" Glynn. "Lord, I'd get sick of them!" she remembered, "I'd say 'Fella, why don't you put that guitar down?' 'Oh, oh, Miss Harvey, don't say that, let him learn!' I said, 'Well you-all worryin' me.' I go to bed and leave 'em sittin' up there. And he [Johnson] be up there plunkin' on the guitar: plunka-lunka! Plunka-lunka! My husband couldn't play but one old tune he learned in the hills, but [at least] he [could] play it."[30]

Something of those first steps may have been retained in the dampened monotone bass line heard in "Last Fair Deal Gone Down" (Fig. 5).

---

[23] LaVere 1990, 7
[24] LaVere, 11
[25] LaVere, 7; Guralnick 1982, 28-29
[26] Calt and Wardlow 1989, 42
[27] Guralnick 1982, 29
[28] LaVere, 5, 9
[29] Calt and Wardlow, 42
[30] Calt and Wardlow 1989, 42-43

Fig. 5 – Robert Johnson, "Last Fair Deal Gone Down"

Open A Tuning; Down 1/2 Step:
(low to high) E♭–A♭–E♭–A♭–C–E♭

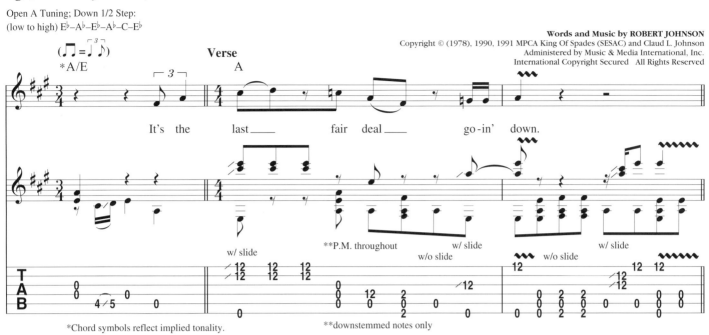

*Chord symbols reflect implied tonality.   **downstemmed notes only

"Come On in My Kitchen" may also have begun from this early period. A melodic precedent of "Kitchen" is Leroy Carr's 1928 smash hit "How Long How Long Blues," which friends recalled[31] Johnson knowing upon its release. It is likely that Johnson was playing the bass pattern heard on his 1936 record (Fig. 6) as early as 1929; in this piece and context, however, the quarter notes function in imitation of Leroy Carr's piano style rather than as a remnant of Johnson's early guitar efforts. Nor was he alone in covering this song at so young an age. Muddy Waters, in his later years, recalled "How Long" as the first blues he learned[32] while a teenager on Stovall's plantation.

Fig. 6 – Robert Johnson, "Come On in My Kitchen"

Open A Tuning, Down 1/2 Step; Capo II:
(low to high) E♭–A♭–E♭–A♭–C–E♭

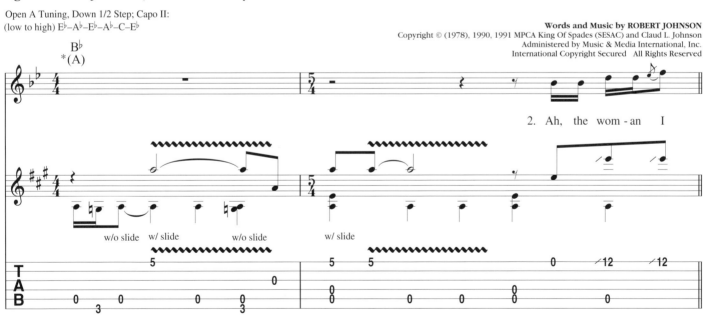

* Symbols in parentheses represent chord names (implied tonality) respective to capoed guitar.
  Symbols above reflect implied tonality. Capoed fret is "0" in Tab.

---

[31] LaVere, 9 ♪
[32] Palmer 1981, 111

To blow the harmonica while strumming his guitar, Johnson fashioned a rack with heavy baling wire.[33] If one was to hear him around 1929, one would expect him to play harmonica solos over a spare "plunka-lunka" bass line (similar to the "country two-beat" heard on Charlie Patton's "You Gonna Need Somebody When You Gone to Die") on a guitar. It is unlikely he would have attempted a piano boogie pattern quite yet, mostly because such piano traits would be developed a little later, as will be shown in Chapter 4. To his credit, Johnson sought tips for improvement from bluesmen like Willie Brown and Willie Moore (later Elizabeth Glynn's second husband), and he took note of the arrivals of Charlie Patton in early 1930, and of Son House later that summer, around Lula and Robinsonville.

Like many other Delta bluesmen at that time, Johnson probably knew he had to rise to Patton's level of accomplished musicianship if he wished to earn his living through music. Patton could strum his guitar in standard tuning as well as play slide in open G tuning. He could play blues in a variety of tempi, as well as sacred music in either the restrained Protestant manner or in the frenetic sanctified style. Other bluesmen copied Patton's "Pony Blues" or "Screamin' or Hollerin' the Blues," yet Johnson learned "Banty Rooster Blues" and "You Gonna Need Somebody When You Gone to Die" to later recast them as "Traveling Riverside Blues" and "Last Fair Deal Gone Down," respectively. He was even able to insert a few Patton guitar licks into some later songs. For instance, the bare single note, plucked just before the fourth beat of the first measure of the dominant V phrase of "Terraplane Blues" (Fig. 7A), shares the same accentuating function as Patton's sharp, single strum at the same place in the 12-measure blues chorus of "Screamin' and Hollerin' the Blues" (Fig. 7B).

Fig. 7A – Robert Johnson, "Terraplane Blues"

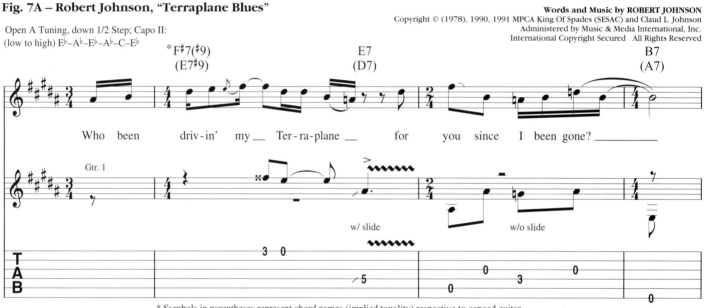

* Symbols in parentheses represent chord names (implied tonality) respective to capoed guitar.
Symbols above reflect implied tonality. Capoed fret is "0" in Tab.

Fig. 7B – Charlie Patton, "Screamin' & Hollerin' the Blues"

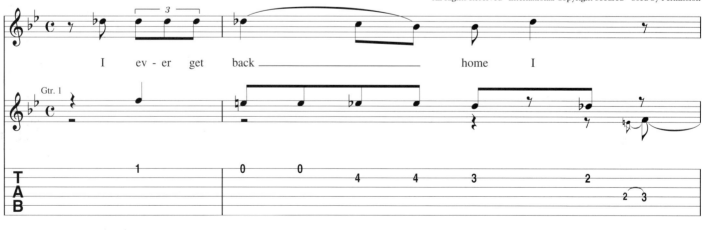

---

[33] LaVere, 9

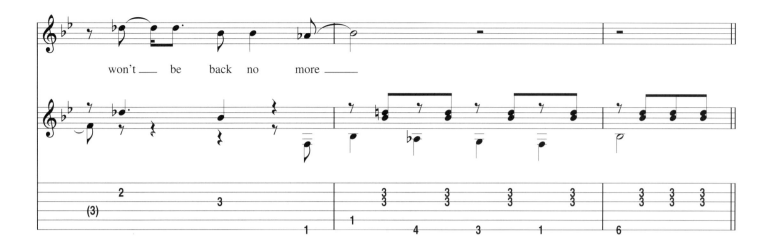

won't ___ be   back   no   more ____

The First Chance I Get

During the summer of 1930, Patton was asked by his label, Paramount Records, to come to its studio in Grafton, Wisconsin for a recording session and to bring additional musicians of his choice from Mississippi.[34] Patton arrived at the session with piano player (and former girlfriend) Louise Johnson (no relation to Robert), Willie Brown, and a recent arrival to the upper Delta area, Son House. Robert Johnson may have known of this trip—a trip which could have awakened his ambition for making commercial records. Almost forty years later, in 1969, Elizabeth Glynn Moore[35] remembered Johnson telling her, "The first chance I get I'm goin' to New York—they tell me there's a good place up there where you just make a record and you can get lots of money for it." If Johnson said this to her after Patton's 1930 trip to Paramount, it is likely he thought New York was the place to go, since all Paramount record labels bore the legend "New York Recorded Laboratories." If whom Johnson referred to as "they" were Patton, Willie Brown, Son House, and Louise Johnson, they did not correct his thinking that they went to New York and received money for making records. Each musician got about $50 per three-minute performance—the same amount made per year from sharecropping after expenses were paid at the end of a harvest. For the eight three-minute performances he recorded, Son House should have been entitled to four hundred dollars; later in life, he said he got forty dollars, which he nonetheless considered good money in the Delta for 1930.[36]

Johnson's ambitions for the future were brighter than his immediate prospects. He had married Virginia Travis in February 1929; he was a few months shy of eighteen at the time and she was fifteen. But the union ended tragically in April 1930 when she and the baby she was delivering both died during labor.[37] Nothing seemed to improve when Robert moved back to his mother and stepfather's home. Dusty Willis's mood must have been grim throughout the record 102-day drought that ruined his early cotton crop and stunted the late one. Perhaps he became more grim upon finding himself with a stepson who would rather play guitar at night than assist in the fields during the day. Local musicians were well aware of Willis's exasperation with Johnson. Son House later recalled, "His parents just didn't want him 'round those kinda parties, but when he get a chance, he get out the kitchen window after he think they gone to sleep and he'd come to where (we) was."[38]

---

[34] Komara 1997a, 8
[35] Calt and Wardlow 1989, 44
[36] House to Lester, 1965, 41
[37] LaVere, 9; Guralnick, 29
[38] House to Lester, 41

It seems House shared Willis's impatience with Johnson, although for different reasons. In the fall of 1930, Charlie Patton moved some ways south to the Holly Ridge area[39] between Greenville on the west and Indianola and Greenwood on the east. House and Willie Brown stayed in the Robinsonville region to earn what money they could from the local sharecroppers after the meager harvest. House later remembered regularly seeing Johnson at the frolics, and having to shoo him away from his and Brown's guitars during breaks,[40] perhaps fearing that Johnson would break a string. Patton was a rare exception among Delta bluesmen in encouraging younger musicians; House was among the distrustful norm.

Perhaps due to these problems at home and the lack of continuing musical instruction around Robinsonville, Johnson may have felt the need to leave his parents in the Delta for a place where music was played year-round, not just at harvest time. Hazlehurst seemed a logical place; it was his birthplace (where he still may have found several family friends and perhaps even his biological father, Noah Johnson), and its local industries, with their regular pay periods, enabled workers to support live music. So in late 1930, Johnson went to Hazlehurst, most likely by taking an Illinois Central train at Robinsonville and riding through Jackson.

Delta swamp, north Leflore County, MS

Return to Hazlehurst

Hazlehurst in 1930 must have seemed a little unreal to newcomers. Times in the Delta were so hard with the great drought that summer and the Mississippi River flood three years earlier that the current Great Depression was hardly news to the sharecroppers; they had been living in an economic depression for some years. Compared to the Delta and the rest of the country, however, Hazlehurst was becoming rather prosperous. In addition to being a county seat and an important Illinois Central Railroad stop, it was also a focal point for regional lumber camps. More recently, Highway 51 was being constructed through Jackson and McComb to New Orleans. The segment leading to and from Hazlehurst needed and attracted a fresh supply of laborers. Unlike Delta sharecroppers who were scattered across expansive plantations near the fields they tilled, the Hazlehurst workers formed a large, residential, regularly paid work force who could support music on a year-round basis.

Enter Ike Zinnerman

It is not known if Johnson took a laboring job when he first returned to Hazlehurst as an adult, or whether he found his true father Noah Johnson. It is generally accepted that early in his stay he found a musical mentor identified by LaVere[41] as Ike Zinnerman. Under Zinnerman's tutelage, he likely began to cultivate various styles of blues outside of those he heard in the Delta.

Ike Zinnerman, from LaVere's research, was about ten years older than Johnson and had been born in Grady, Alabama. It seems he had been playing blues for some years before meeting Johnson, and he apparently told his wife he learned to play guitar while sitting atop tombstones in graveyards,[42] perhaps to mask the years of practice behind his proficiency. A photograph[43] shows him to be carefree and confident. Unfortunately, he made no commercial records nor left vanity discs; such records could have shown what he was capable of demonstrating to young Johnson. A fair guess would be a review of the standard and open-chord tunings used by Delta guitarists, some practical tips on how to study records and thus derive guitar technique and alternate tunings, and an introduction to the latest commercial blues coming out on records. If these lessons were indeed taught by Zinnerman, they were well retained by his only known pupil.

There can be little doubt that Zinnerman made much use of blues records while teaching his protègè. Although he had the ambition of someday making records while living in the Delta, in Hazlehurst Johnson may have learned how to use other musicians' current records as study aids. He may have also recognized the recording medium as a means of disseminating his own music.

[39] Calt and Wardlow 1988, 229

[40] House to Lester, 41

[41] LaVere, 1990, 11

[42] LaVere, 11

[43] LaVere, 10

The Early Blues on Record

The first blues record, "Crazy Blues," by Cincinnati singer Mamie Smith, was released by Okeh Records in 1920; its high sales indicated a commercial market for records by black musicians for black buyers.[44] The resulting "race records" industry was largely dominated by women singers such as Bessie Smith, Alberta Hunter, Ida Cox, and countless others throughout the 1920s. But in 1926, Paramount Records introduced a rural Texas bluesman, Blind Lemon Jefferson, whose first records, including "Black Snake Moan," stirred the record industry's interest in rustic blues from the southern states.[45] It can be safely said that largely due to Jefferson's continuing success on records, Charlie Patton and his generation of Mississippi Delta bluesmen enjoyed recording sessions of their own.

When Delta blacks wanted to hear music, they went to church for sacred hymns or to a juke or picnic for blues. With the lack of electricity across the plantations, many blacks saved enough money—or sometimes chipped in with others—for a wind-up record player. Records could be purchased by mail order ads in the *Chicago Defender* newspaper or at the artists' appearances (like Joe LaVene selling Charlie Patton 78s at picnics[46]). It seems (according to research by Gayle Wardlow[47] and Jeff Todd Titon[48]) that women were more likely than men to buy Victrolas and records, and their tastes ran as deep in sacred music as in blues.

H.C. Speir

With a fair-sized population in high concentration, Hazlehurst blacks had available to them a greater variety of music than the sharecroppers in the Delta. Also relying on windup phonographs, Hazlehurstans had access to records not only in their own town, but also in Jackson, a few railroad stops north on the Illinois Central line. The best place in Jackson to buy "race records" was Speir's Music on Farish St. Henry C. Speir, a white man, opened his store in 1925 in the black part of Jackson and served the requests of his customers. A 1929 photograph of Speir's shows portable Victrola boxes piled on the left and Columbia and Victor posters hanging in the back.[49] In addition to Columbia and Victor releases, those from Paramount, Gennett, and Vocalion could also be purchased there. If a blues or sacred performer had made records, chances were that copies were on sale at Speir's.

Whenever customers showed interest in a popular Mississippi musician who had yet to make records, Speir was quick to refer that artist to the record labels. Today, Speir is known more for being a Mississippi talent scout for the record industry than as a Jackson businessman, although much of the reasoning behind what he called his "talent brokering" was to increase record sales at his store.[50] Over the fifteen years he scouted black talent, he never took a commission from the labels on sales of his discoveries' records. He simply had enough faith in his retail receipts from selling 300 to 600 records (out of a stock of 3000) on a single Saturday.[51] But he did have to make sure the artists he sent were topnotch, and most of them were. Tommy Johnson and Ishmon Bracey who, along with Charlie Patton, were among his greatest blues discoveries, recorded first at a Victor record session in Memphis in 1928. Yet Victor always seemed to want expensive test demonstration discs for audition. Speir did keep a recording machine and microphone in his store for such use, but it seemed he wanted to use it as little as possible. A label that he found easier to work with was Paramount, which was always happy to accept his recommendations without a test disc or qualification.[52] In 1929, when Charlie Patton became a best-selling artist for Paramount on the order of Lemon Jefferson, his success enhanced Speir's reputation in the eyes of Paramount's owner, the Wisconsin Chair Company. In April 1930, Wisconsin Chair offered to sell him the label but Speir turned down the offer, partly because he had his spare capital invested in an oil scheme with other Jackson investors.[53] He did, however, continue to work with the record labels. In October 1930, he hosted an Okeh Records visit to Jackson to record the local blues, sacred, and white hillbilly talent. Throughout the Okeh Jackson sessions, he worked with his chosen artists to prepare and, if need be, develop material for commercial sale.

---

[44] Dixon and Godrich 1970, 9-10
[45] Dixon and Godrich 1970, 34-35
[46] Evans 1987, 152
[47] Howse and Phillips 1995, 41
[48] Jeff Todd Titon 1977, 271-276
[49] Wardlow 1994, 15; Wardlow 1998, 134
[50] Wardlow 1994, 13
[51] Wardlow 1994, 23
[52] Wardlow 1994, 13
[53] Wardlow 1994, 25

This commercial aspect in early records of Mississippi music may be disconcerting to those who seek traditional folk mannerisms or personal artistic expressions in them. To be sure, they are filled with such mannerisms and expressions, yet the obvious tailoring of music and words according to previous hit songs and records cannot be ignored. Charlie Patton, for example, borrowed much material from Ma Rainey's "Booze and Blues" to write "Tom Rushen Blues" for his first session in 1929, and then the following year he all but plagiarized the Mississippi Sheiks' smash hit "Sitting on Top of the World" for his "Some Summer Day." Bukka White, who was born in Houston, MS a year earlier than Robert Johnson (1910) and who made his recording debut in 1930 (on the recommendation of Ralph Lembo, Speir's rival talent scout), pandered no less to buyers' expectations. His two sacred sides released by Victor, "I Am in the Heavenly Way" and "Promise True and Grand," are arranged in the style of Blind Willie Johnson, the leading sacred recording musician of the time—with slide guitar accompaniment, a woman assisting on vocals, and brisk tempos. Unlike Willie Johnson's releases, White's Victor 78s sold poorly, and today original copies are extremely rare. Nonetheless, Patton and White's commercial mindfulness towards the public suggest tradition not as a "handing down" from one musician to another, but as a "handing over" to a musician "stealing" successful material. In this way, "covers" of hit records were produced, with few or no adjustments in the melody and accompaniment.

There is a chance that Robert Johnson visited Speir's store in Jackson in 1930 or 1931 and gained some understanding of what level of talent it took to perform on records. He may have heard about the Okeh visit that fall, and in the following winter may have learned of Speir sending a Bentonia bluesman named Skip James to the Paramount studio "up north." And, he may have heard of and listened to some of the latest releases of the time. These could have included not only those that Patton, Son House, Willie Brown, and Louise Johnson made on their northern trip the previous summer, but also those by guitarists in other blues centers in other states, including Blind Blake, Tampa Red, and Lonnie Johnson. Not only were their records the sources of melodic themes in the eight-, twelve-, or sixteen-measure blues, but also of guitar fills, licks, and tags for use in any song. Perhaps with Zinnerman's help, Johnson apparently learned how to discern what guitar tuning was being used in person or on record, and how each were used in the songs he heard in the Delta and the new ones in Jackson and Hazlehurst.

Blind Blake

Blind Blake in 1930 was a Paramount recording star, yet oddly little else is certain about the rest of his life. It is believed, from Paramount ads and booklets of the time, that Blake's first name was Arthur and that he supposedly was born in Jacksonville, Florida. When and how he died still remains a mystery. Yet the versatility of his musicianship was captured on Paramount releases from his first hit, "West Coast Blues," in 1926 through his last release in 1932.

If he was indeed from Jacksonville, a city that seems more a part of Georgia than of Florida, his performing style was clean and professional. His singing, if slightly nasal, was free of regional traces, and his guitar technique in standard tuning was more adaptable to different kinds of blues than the regional practices of the Delta and east Texas. For example, his 1927 record "Georgia Bound" uses the twelve-measure blues melody of the folk song "Betty and Dupree" in an AAB lyric scheme, but it is sung without folk inflections and is accompanied with snappy guitar licks and fills. It is likely Johnson had Blake's "Georgia Bound" treatment in mind while preparing "From Four Until Late," for he too performs the same traditional melody with words and guitar accompaniment to appeal to farm and city people alike. But there are some important differences between the two records. Blake plays in alternating low octave tones like a stride piano player, while Johnson plays with a straight common-time bass monotone in the manner of Leroy Carr or a big-city pianist. Both use different fill-licks, Johnson's being more harmonic. Yet they seem to use a similar chorus turnaround that ends on the dominant scale tone.

Another Blake record, "One Time Blues," to be presented in chapter 4, if not heard in itself by Johnson, would nevertheless have an indirect influence through the subsequent treatments of the theme by others on songs like "Kokomo Blues."

Tampa Red

Tampa Red came from the same region of the South as Blind Blake and, like him, established himself in the mid-1920s as a blues guitar entertainer. Born Hudson Whittaker in the early 1900s in Georgia, he acquired his nickname from having been raised in Tampa, Florida and having red hair. But it was in Chicago in 1928 that he made his early fame by recording, with pianist Thomas A. "Georgia Tom" Dorsey (of Ma Rainey's backup group), "Tight Like That" for Vocalion. Splitting the 12-measure blues chorus into a 4-measure verse and an 8-measure refrain, this particular blues melody had appeared in 1925 on Charlie Jackson's "Shake That Thing." But it became widely established through the catchy "Tight Like That" record with its risqué lyrics and breezy manner, and its overall style came to be labeled "hokum." The record's commercial success yielded several "sequels" by Tampa Red and Dorsey as well as countless cover versions and appropriations by other performers. Among them were "Going Back to Texas" by Memphis Minnie and Kansas Joe McCoy, and a few years later, "Step It Up and Go" by Blind Boy Fuller. Doubtless Robert Johnson in 1929 knew Tampa Red's version of "Tight Like That," as seven years later he uses its turnaround figure (Fig. 8) in his "Last Fair Deal Gone Down." In addition, the fame of "Tight Like That" extended into popular catchphrases. Louis Armstrong, in December 1928, punned with the "Tight Like That" title in a patter-prelude before launching into one of the greatest trumpet solos in jazz on "Tight Like This."

Fig. 8 – Robert Johnson, "Last Fair Deal Gone Down"

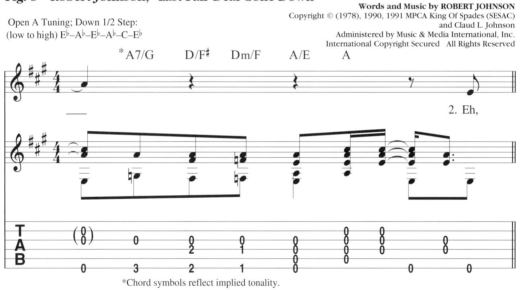

Tampa Red continued his success with more hokum records, among them "What Is It That Tastes Like Gravy" in 1929, that used a sixteen-measure AABA form with four phrases of four measures each. This tune would also become closely identified with hokum blues and would remain in blues practice through 1941 with the performances of Big Bill Broonzy and Washboard Sam. Johnson would play the "Gravy" melody (perhaps better known to him as "Every Jug Stands on Its Own Bottom," as Broonzy recorded it) as "They're Red Hot," in standard tuning. One Johnson commentator, Bob Groom,[54] has said that a half brother of Johnson's, Red Johnson, was remembered to have been strongly associated with "They're Red Hot," but it is uncertain whether "Red Johnson" was indeed a half brother or merely one of Robert's pseudonyms. The wide use of this melody on hit records from 1929 on nevertheless suggests that Johnson began developing "They're Red Hot" while at Hazlehurst, adding more lyrics from time to time.

[54] May/June 1976, 12

Lonnie Johnson

Although he was not related to Lonnie Johnson, Robert could uncannily imitate the older and more famous musician. Lonnie Johnson was born in 1894 in New Orleans, but moved in 1925 to St. Louis and became a leader in that city's blues scene. His records with Louis Armstrong in 1927 and with fellow guitarist Eddie Lang confirmed his professional guitar skills, while his entertaining vocal records sold well with the general public everywhere.

Robert Johnson apparently chose to copy Lonnie Johnson's vocal records like "Blue Ghost Blues" with its lyric "Lord I'm sinking down." Another blues of this type, "Life Saver Blues" provided the basis for Robert's "Drunken Hearted Man" and "Malted Milk." Yet in his imitation, he did not stop with the distinctive melody and the self-deprecating lyrics, but also (perhaps with the aid of Ike Zinnerman) discerned the open strings and fretted tones on the record to figure out Lonnie Johnson's drop-D tuning (low to high, D–A–D–G–B–E), and drop-D/drop-G tuning (D–G–D–G–B–E).

One chord that Lonnie Johnson uses in the tonic phrase fills of "Life Saver Blues" is the tonic seventh chord (I7), usually with the third and fifth tones omitted and the seventh tone inverted underneath the tonic. The dominant seventh (V7) chord is basic to Western harmony, but the I7 serves a leading-tone function in the specific blues contexts of the instrumental fills. This is true of the blues practices of the time in the city and in the country. In his own records, Robert Johnson would use the I7 chord in his fills as a common elemental bond in his sophisticated and rustic blues alike.

The success of his imitation lingered for more than forty years, when Hazlehurst old-timers recalled a "Robert Lonnie Johnson" who could perform like the famous Lonnie Johnson (LaVere, 12). The drop-D tuning (and its related drop-D/drop-G tuning) may have enabled him to disguise himself in a musical persona, with much of the same protection from trouble that his nicknames provided. If so, Johnson may have seriously begun pursuing other alternate guitar tunings to develop other musical guises.

CHAPTER THREE

Johnson and the Classic Delta Guitar Masters 1931-1934

The Crossroads Myth

The legend today most associated with Robert Johnson tells of him selling his soul to the devil at a Delta crossroads for improved guitar skills; this occurred at about the time he was studying with Ike Zinnerman in Hazlehurst. The pegs on which this yarn is spun are two quotes by Son House in his old age 35 years after the supposed deal.

The first remark was to Julius Lester[55]: "He stayed [away from Robinsonville], looked like to me about six months. Willie [Brown] and I were playing again out at a little place east of Robinsonville called Banks, Mississippi. We were playing there one Saturday night and, somebody came in through the door. Who but him! He had a guitar swinging on his back. I said 'Bill!' He said, 'Huh?' I said, 'Look who's coming through the door.' He looked and said, 'Yeah, little Robert.' I said, 'And he's got a guitar.' And Willie and I laughed about it. Robert finally wiggled through the crowd and got to where we were. He spoke, and I said, 'Well, boy, you still got a guitar, huh? What do you do with that thing? You can't do nothing with it.' He said, 'Well, I'll tell you what.' I said, 'What?' He said, 'Let me have your seat a minute.' So I said, 'All right, and you better do something with it, too,' and I winked my eye at Willie. So he sat down there and finally got started. And man! He was so good! When he finished, all our mouths were standing open. I said, 'Well, ain't that fast! He's gone now!'"

The other quote, also from 1965, was made to Pete Welding,[56] who includes it after House's description of Johnson's homecoming: "He must have sold his soul to the devil to play like that." Welding wrote that House "suggested [it] in all seriousness," but it is open to doubt whether the old bluesman said it out of envy, disdain, or awe. Regardless, this quote apparently was the kernel from which the devil myth sprouted. By 1968 Eric Clapton, then with the rock group Cream, sang in his cover of Johnson's "Cross Road Blues": "I went down to the crossroads, fell down on my knees (repeat)/ I saw the devil, I went up, and I said, 'Take me if you please.'" Johnson had sung "I asked the Lord to have mercy, save poor Bob if you please."

Believing the crossroads myth hampers an understanding of Johnson's music, and ascribes a naive sense of religion to him and House that, quite possibly, neither had. The only published recollection of Johnson even being near a church was Evie House's memory of him as a young teenager entertaining his classmates with his harmonica outside a Methodist church schoolhouse.[57] For that matter, the only tune Johnson recorded that could be regarded as sacred in origin is "The Last Fair Deal Gone Down," which shares its melody with "I'm Gonna Do All I Can" (Chapter 1, Fig. 3). As for Son House, he is typically

Crossroads gas station, Highway 6, Panola County, MS

Photo by Edward Komara

described as one who "vacillated over the course of a long lifetime between the Bible and the bottle."[58] From his recordings of the 1930s, the 1940s, and his 1960s rediscovery, House seemed reconciled with the purities and temptations in life and with the sacred and secular types of music associated respectively with them. But he may have wavered between wholehearted spiritual faith and cynicism when his faith was abused by religious leaders. House was ironic in singing his "Preaching the Blues" (1930) to a workaday field holler: "I'm gonna get me religion, I'm gonna join the Baptist Church (repeat)/I'm gonna be a Baptist preacher and I sure won't have to work."

---

[55] Lester 1965, 41-42
[56] Welding 1966, 76
[57] Calt and Wardlow 1988, 42
[58] Evans, 41, in Oliver 1989

The Influence of Son House

Eddie "Son" House Jr. was born on the Riverton plantation near Clarksdale, Mississippi, ostensibly in 1902, although family and close associates believe he may have been born as early as 1886. House, in his old age, privately admitted he lied about his birth date to an employer, but he never revealed by how many years the true difference was.[59] As he told Julius Lester,[60] he grew up in Louisiana and spent many of his working years through 1927 drifting among jobs between New Orleans and St. Louis. In 1927, he heard Willie Wilson play bottleneck slide on a guitar in Matson, a hamlet just south of Clarksdale, and the following year, with Wilson's help, he took up bottleneck slide guitar himself. Before long, he was playing blues at jukes and at one of them in 1928 he killed a man in self-defense. He was duly arrested and sentenced for a term at Parchman Penitentiary in the Delta and two years later was released.[61] He then headed north to Lula where he had an aunt, and there he met Charlie Patton.[62]

Patton is often referred to by critics as a mentor for House, and sometimes he is even cited as an influence. More likely, Patton was a sponsor, since he had never met or heard House until the latter's arrival in Lula; but once he did, he invited the new musician in town to join him in making records. In the summer of 1930, perhaps as late as August or September, House went with Patton, Willie Brown, and Louise Johnson to the Paramount studio in Grafton, Wisconsin. There, he cut eight songs for four double-sided releases under his own name. "Dry Spell Blues," parts one and two, described the drought ravaging the South that summer. "Mississippi County Farm Blues" and  an unissued "Walking Blues,"[63] were based on melodies by Lemon Jefferson, whose death House had learned of from producer Art Laibley during the session.[64] "Preaching the Blues" and "My Black Mama," like "Dry Spell," were long, two-sided blues based on axe-song chants. The remaining issued song, "Clarksdate Moan," is lyrics about Clarksdale sung to the melody of Patton's "Pony Blues."

After the session, House decided to stay in Robinsonville, in part to perform with Willie Brown, with whom he had become a friend during the trip to Grafton. House may have been an unknown at the time of his move to Robinsonville and his first encounter with Robert Johnson, but his name quickly became known through the force of his public performances and the publicity of his records. Paramount released its House 78s from October 1930 through the next twelve months;[65] this time coincided with Robert Johnson's study in Hazlehurst.

Johnson returned to Robinsonville sometime in 1931, most likely during or just after harvest time when the local farmers had money to spend. One's imagination can run wild speculating what Johnson may have played that night in Banks for House and Brown. Did he play "Cross Road Blues," or "Sweet Home Chicago," and in the ways he recorded them in 1936? If he did, the legend would be truly astounding. He more likely played "Malted Milk," "They're Red Hot," or an early version of "Last Fair Deal Gone Down," which, however lesser they seem to his later achievements, are still remarkable improvements over what Robinsonville people recalled him playing previously. Yet for all his progress, Johnson must have wished to move on to additional, and profitable, musical models. He probably recognized House as a certifiable Delta blues star with four Paramount releases to his credit; he may have even seen House's name on Paramount dealer's lists[66] at Speir's in Jackson. There is no doubt he found much commercial and musical value in House's blues, as five years later he recorded his own versions of "My Black Mama" (retitled "Walking Blues") and "Preaching Blues."

---

[59] Waterman 1989, 48
[60] Lester 1965, 38-40
[61] Wilson 1966, 3
[62] Lester 1965, 40
[63] Komara 1997b
[64] Wilson 1966, 5; Calt and Wardlow 1988, 219
[65] Vreede 1971
[66] like the October 1930 list in Vreede 1971

The melody of "My Black Mama," which House later attributed to James McCoy of Lyon, a small town near Clarksdale, is akin to a field chant—the axe fall presumably occurring at the rests at the beginning of each measure (Chapter 1, Fig. 1). He adapts the chant to the twelve-measure form by singing the whole lyric to the tonic chord in measures 1–4, repeating the first half of the phrase to a subdominant IV chord in measures 5–8, then giving the remainder to the V and I chords in measures 9–12. His guitar accompaniment is a thumbed bass-string strum in open G tuning (and a capo on fret 2), with the fingers picking the ascending motif fretted with a bottleneck (Fig. 9), and the thumb snapping the fifth string during the IV chord (meas. 5–6) of each chorus.

Figure 9 – Son House, "My Black Mama"
Open G tuning, Capo II

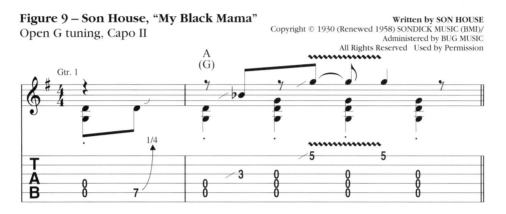

In his 1936 rendition, Johnson retains many of House's features, including the thumbed strum on the lower strings, the fingerpicking on the treble strings, and in a later chorus, the snapped beats during the IV chord. However, instead of playing the ascending bottleneck motif, he plays only an ornamental pitch on the top string. He does retain House's twelve-measure AA lyric structure, but he accelerates the tempo with each passing chorus, building a momentum not present in House's original.

Johnson also recorded in 1936 a cover of House's "Preaching the Blues." House in 1930 apparently tuned the guitar to an open D chord, yet as in open G tuning he continues to strum the bass strings while picking the treble motif:

Figure 10A – Son House, "Preaching the Blues"

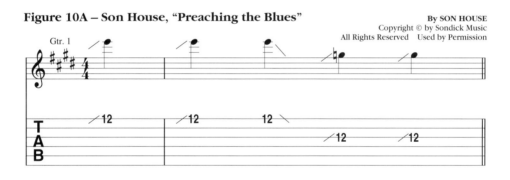

Johnson follows much the same practice, except he adds a couple of pitches (the ♭7th scale tone and the tonic octave) to create a descending run motif:

Figure 10B – Robert Johnson, "Preachin' Blues (Up Jumped the Devil)"
Open E Tuning; Down 1/2 Step:
(low to high) E♭–B♭–E♭–G♮–B♭–E♭

*downstemmed notes only

In both treatments, the lyric scheme is in a twelve-measure AAB form. House, however, declaims his lyrics in a work song manner with an axe-fall rest at the beginning of each phrase. In seemingly modern touches, Johnson begins his lyrical phrases on the pickup (fourth beat) in the measure preceding where each phrase was expected to start. What makes Johnson's version so fearsome for musicians and listeners alike is his fast tempo. He executes many difficult guitar licks, one of which (Fig. 10C) is a musical quote from House's version of "Pony Blues" (which attests to Johnson's accurate musical memory, as House would not record "Pony Blues" until 1941, three years after Johnson's death).

Figure 10C – Robert Johnson, "Preachin' Blues (Up Jumped the Devil)"

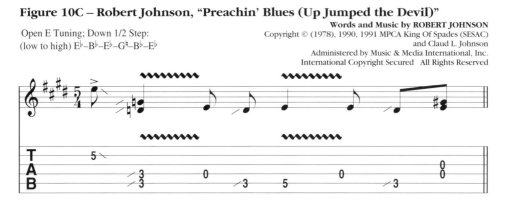

Due to the musical discipline Johnson needed to achieve these technical accomplishments, he likely learned House's blues after his study with Ike Zinnerman. Despite the claims of some writers and publicists, House, after his 1964 rediscovery, never really acknowledged that he taught anything specific to Johnson, except to warn him about talking to women during performance breaks.[67] Yet in 1931, Johnson seemed to be developing his amazing ability to figure out how to play what he was hearing live or on record, and then outdo his model by inserting quotes from other blues. Elizabeth Glynn, despite her impatience during Johnson's early lessons in the late 1920s, admitted later in her life to Wardlow that he came "over (better than) Son House to my idea of playin'."[68]

Honing the Slide Sound on the Middle Strings

Two additional slide guitar pieces may have been picked up by Johnson at this time, perhaps to hone his bottleneck technique. One may have been "Come On in My Kitchen." The melody appeared on records as early as 1925, when Ida Cox, with "Papa" Charlie Jackson accompanying, sang it to the words "How Long Daddy How Long." It was used to commercial success by Leroy Carr with Scrapper Blackwell in 1928 as "How Long How Long," a record which Johnson's neighbors remember him learning the year following its release. But in 1930, the Mississippi Sheiks, in their first session, played the melody with fiddle and guitar as "Sitting on Top of the World." That record became a huge hit for the Okeh label and the Sheiks, who would re-record it in 1932 for Paramount. For all its popularity, the Sheiks' treatment  seemed curiously rustic, even backward. During the opening chorus, Lonnie Chatman performs the theme on fiddle with an unrosined bow, while Walter Vincson alternated plucked bass tones with strummed chords:

Figure 11A – Mississippi Sheiks, "Sitting on Top of the World"

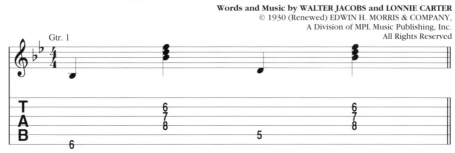

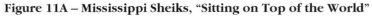

[67] Lester 1965, 42
[68] Calt and Wardlow 1989, 43

Johnson, in his 1936 recording, seems to copy the Sheiks. In the first half of the first chorus, with his slide technique and humming voice, he gives an approximate imitation of Lonnie Chatman's fiddle; however, he replaces Vincson's accompaniment with a thumbed bass line likely lifted from Leroy Carr's piano part in "How Long How Long":

Figure 11B – Robert Johnson, "Come On in My Kitchen"

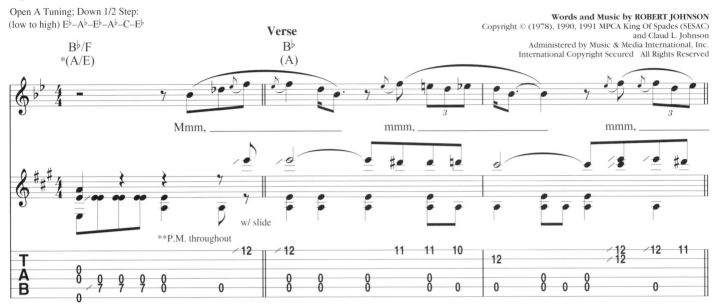

* Symbols in parentheses represent chord names (implied tonality) respective to capoed guitar.
Symbols above reflect implied tonality. Capoed fret is "0" in Tab.
** downstemmed notes only

Another record that Johnson possibly studied at this time was "Roll and Tumble Blues" by "Hambone" Willie Newburn, issued by Okeh in 1929. Although Newburn recorded the song in Atlanta, Georgia, he may have learned it in Mississippi. Sleepy John Estes, the renowned blues singer and guitarist from Brownsville, Tennessee, late in his life recalled playing with Newburn in medicine shows in Como, located on the northeast edge of the Mississippi Delta.[69] Considering some melodic similarity of "Roll and Tumble Blues" to Patton's "Banty Rooster Blues," Newburn may have learned the song in Mississippi, perhaps around Como. Newburn's distinguishing contribution to the song was a guitar lick on the middle strings, which Johnson replicated (see Fig. 12) on his version of this tune called "If I Had Possession Over Judgment Day," and in the accompaniment to "Traveling Riverside Blues." By learning that lick, he furthered his technique on the middle strings of the open A-tuned guitar in addition to the bass and top strings.

Fig. 12 – Robert Johnson, "If I Had Possession Over Judgment Day,"
repeated fills—lick from Newburn's "Roll and Tumble Blues"

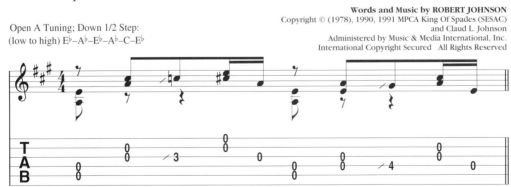

---

[69] Lornell 1975, 42

Johnny Temple

In 1932, Johnson continued to shuttle between the Delta, Jackson, and Hazlehurst. He added to these regular stops Hattiesburg, the seat of Forrest County. Like Hazlehurst, it offered much labor on the railroad, in the lumber camps, and the Highway 11 road crews. The town was accessible on the Gulf and Ship Island Railroad linking Jackson and Gulfport. By Johnson's time, the railroad had become part of the vast Illinois Central network of Mississippi railways.

That same year in Jackson, Johnson met a young singer and guitarist named Johnny Temple. As he recalled to Gayle Wardlow in the late 1960s, Temple knew Johnson only as "R.L.," who would frequently stop in Jackson while traveling between Hattiesburg and the Delta.[70] Apparently, the two young bluesmen swapped songs, for Temple would record the Son House "My Black Mama" melody as "Lead Pencil Blues" in 1935, and Johnson would base two songs on those of Temple's mentor, Nehemiah "Skip" James.

Skip James

James was born in 1902 in Yazoo City and raised in nearby Bentonia. He began playing guitar seriously in the mid-1920s when a fellow Bentonian, Henry Stuckey, showed him a D minor tuning (D–A–D–F–A–D).[71] This tuning wasn't unique to Bentonia; Bukka White would also tune in D minor, but would habitually fret the F♯ on the third string to keep from playing in the D minor key.[72] But James thought and performed differently. He called the D minor tuning "cross-note," perhaps recognizing that the F pitch was the pivotal difference between major and minor scales. Using some of Stuckey's repertory, James cultivated a body of songs and blues in D minor, accompanying himself by plucking the guitar strings in hollow-sounding intervals of octaves and tenths. James would also add the major 3rd to his D minor tuning for a few major key songs like "Four O'Clock Blues," while still retaining his fingerplucking technique.

Temple first met James in 1929 in Jackson when James would frequently catch an Illinois Central train in Bentonia and make the twenty-five-mile trip to the state capital. The two offered an informal music school in guitar, piano, and fiddle in Jackson. Whatever the number of students they had, they got to know each other rather well.[73] Temple learned much of James's repertory, and it may have been Temple who taught several songs to Joe McCoy. Then enjoying great success with his partner Memphis Minnie and their hit record "Bumble Bee," McCoy was ever on the watch for new material for recording sessions. In late 1930, McCoy recorded James's "Cypress Grove" melody as "Cherry Ball," and four years later did a cover of James's "Devil Got My Woman" as "Evil Devil Woman Blues." In early 1931, James went to Speir's Music for a record audition, and after playing only "Devil Got My Woman," secured himself a Paramount session.[74] He recorded eighteen sides at the company's studios in Grafton, and later despaired over their lack of commercial success, blaming Paramount for insufficient promotion. The truth was that the label's profits were declining due to the Great Depression, and it could no longer run its prominent ads in the Chicago Defender newspaper. By the end of 1931, James was disgusted with the business of music, and left it to study theology in his father's seminary.[75]

Johnson may never have met Skip James, and most likely learned his songs from Johnny Temple. James's records were hard to find even at Speir's store, where its owner had difficulty ordering them.[76] If Johnson did hear a James disc, he should have found much to attract and encourage him. James didn't have a powerful voice, and at the pitch B above middle C and upward he sang in falsetto. Nevertheless, the microphone captured his voice well. Johnson, with his own lean voice, must have felt encouraged by James's vocal audibility on records.

---

[70] Calt and Wardlow 1989, 45

[71] Calt 1994, 88-90; also Wardlow's unpublished notes with Stuckey, 1965

[72] Basiuk 1976, 43

[73] Calt 1994, 122-129

[74] Calt 1994, 134; Guralnick 1966, 12

[75] Guralnick 1966, 14

[76] Calt 1994, 162-163

Stylistically, James stands out from the other Mississippi bluesmen of the 1920s and 1930s in that his music played with the D minor "crossed note" tuning is very harmonic and "vertical." To be sure, the length of his component phrases in "Devil Got My Woman" and other blues can vary from one chorus to the next. Yet what is important is that the harmonies hold together in homophonic chords despite the wide intervals. Thumb-strumming the bass strings and then overlaying with treble licks like Charlie Patton or Son House is something that James would never do. His guitar technique made much use of the bass and middle strings, and in some songs the top string would be used only for ringing ornamental pitches. As foreshadowed in his treatments of blues by Son House and Willie Newburn, Johnson's own technique was coming to have much in common with James's, and the study of the latter's songs would have sharpened his guitar skills even more.

"Yola My Blues Away" and "Hell Hound on My Trail"

For many years, biographers and commentators believed that Johnson's "Hell Hound on My Trail" was based on James's "Devil Got My Woman."[77] To be fair to them, James's "Yola My Blues Away" was not made widely available on reissue records until the 1980s. Nevertheless, "Hell Hound" is a twelve-measure AAB blues, while "Devil" is basically a ten-measure AA (five+five) form whose phrase-pairs are elongated with each chorus. "Yola" is in a twelve-measure form and bears a stronger melodic similarity to "Hell Hound." However, Johnson does use the attachment phrases to each lyric (see Chapter 6 Fig. 33B) in the manner of Temple ("Evil Devil Blues," 1935) and Joe McCoy ("Evil Devil Woman Blues," 1934), although Temple and McCoy retain James's phrase-pair form of "Devil Got My Woman." Interestingly, in "Come On in My Kitchen," Johnson sings "The woman I love/[I] took from my best friend/some joker got lucky/stole her back again," a lyric that James used on "Devil." It is probable that Johnny Temple used the "Devil" attachment phrases and lyrics while teaching "Yola" to Johnson.

Some of the minor-mode inflections of James's guitar sound are noticeably present in Johnson's "Hell Hound" inasmuch as Johnson used open E minor tuning (relative to the D minor tuning of James). Perhaps he lacked the time to study James's D minor guitar sides, for if he had, he would have figured it out like he had with the Lonnie Johnson records. One could argue, though, that E was a better key for Johnson, his strained voice approximating James's falsetto. It is also likely Temple did not understand the tuning from James, since his versions of James's blues are relatively free of minor-mode tones, and hence he taught the song in a garbled fashion to McCoy and Johnson. To his credit, Johnson seems to have absorbed James's fingerplucking technique, and he would come to use it on open and closed harmonic chords in later songs. However, as opposed to James and even most of his other songs, he strums rather than plucks on "Hell Hound."

Hands at the Ready

Another Skip James tune that Johnson later recorded was "22–20 Blues." During the piano portion of his 1931 session, James was asked to record a blues akin to Roosevelt Sykes's "32–20 Blues" of 1930 (not "44 Blues" as commonly believed). He did so, devising his own lyrics and referring to a handgun made by Smith & Wesson. His piano accompaniment was not of a conventional four-bass-beats-per-bar type. Rather, at the beginning of each musical phrase and during the fills between lyrics he provides only short bursts of repeated treble chords. Continuity of this performance relies heavily on the vocal melodic theme.

Judging from his close adaptation of James's lyrics, Johnson must have been familiar with the record. However, he apparently decided to avoid James's mosaic-like style and reset it to the Delta guitar conventions. He used his thumbed-bass technique for the propulsive bass-line, his fingertips for the top-string licks, and his middle-string skills for the fills and chorus

---

77 Not least Guralnick 1982, 36; Obrecht 1990, 64; Calt and Wardlew 1988, 45; Groom 1976 July/Aug., 15.

turnarounds. When Johnson usually borrows a pre-existing blues, he usually is faithful to the accompaniment of the previous version. "32–20 Blues" is a rare instance of him devising a whole new instrumental setting.

Robert Johnson Studio Portrait/Hooks Bros., Memphis, 1935.

The introduction to Johnson's 1936 recording of "32–20 Blues" brings to mind one of the two published photos of him—the 1935 studio portrait. The intro begins with a ringing A7 chord fingered at the eighth and ninth frets, descending stepwise to the V–I cadence before the first chorus. In the studio photo, Johnson frets a basic A7 chord at the fifth fret on a Gibson L-1 guitar (in what should be standard tuning) with his picking thumb resting at the fourth string. This is a portrait of a classic Mississippi guitarslinger, waiting for the cue to play. If the song is to be "32–20 Blues," he need only to readjust his fingers to the eighth and ninth frets for the modified A7 chord, and his picking thumb can begin the opening lick at the fourth string and then start the repeated fifth string note. Although this picture is said to have been taken in 1935, it depicts Johnson as a confident master of all that he learned in Mississippi between 1931 and 1934.

The Last Fair Deal

It may have been in 1932 that "Last Fair Deal Gone Down" took the form in which it is heard on the 1936 record, if the lyrics about the Gulf and Ship Island Railroad are any indication. Despite its references to south Mississippi, the piece seems a musical homage to Charlie Patton, who was still living and performing in the middle Delta between Greenville and Greenwood. Johnson retains Patton's slide part from "You Gonna Need Somebody When You Gone to Die," and when the recorded performance reaches a fevered pitch at the fifth chorus, he launches into a faithful mimic of Patton's incomprehensible diction:

Fig. 13 – Robert Johnson, "Last Fair Deal Gone Down"

Open A Tuning; Down 1/2 Step:
(low to high) E♭–A♭–E♭–A♭–C–E♭

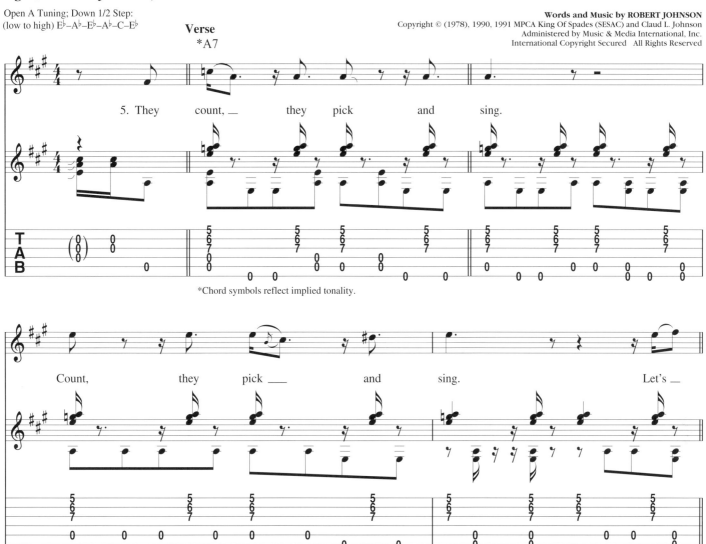

*Chord symbols reflect implied tonality.

Analysis of "Last Fair Deal Gone Down" also indicates the additive manner which Johnson improvised this blues. Usually when jazz musicians improvise on the blues, they alter or even discard the original melody and retain the chords and accompaniment. Johnson and the other classic Delta blues musicians would do the opposite; that is, they would keep the melody but alter the chords and accompaniment. In other words, when Johnson was developing a new number, it seems he would take an existing melody as a template on which he would add or overlay bass figures, ornamental pitches, licks, fills, and new lyrics. Some of the new elements would be freshly created, but others would be taken from other records or from other performers heard live.

"Last Fair Deal Gone Down" has the "I'm Gonna Do All I Can" hymn as its base, with Patton's instrumental accompaniment from his "You Gonna Need Somebody When You Die" underneath the melody. But the added elements should be noted, like Tampa Red's "Tight Like That" turnaround lick quoted at the end of each chorus, and the Patton imitation inserted as a later chorus. Johnson may not have originally conceived of this number in the way he would perform it on record. He may have started with the basic theme, and the more he worked on it, the more he would add new chords and ornaments. The potential for Johnson as a growing musician would be in adding to his collection of musical and lyrical elements, with which he could mix and match in any number of combinations in any song during a live performance. An eventual possibility would be "vertical" harmonic, not linear, embellishments.

Blues Linear and Blues Vertical

Despite his initial stumbling in Robinsonville, Johnson—in a few short years—mastered the Delta blues. The "linear" style that was first noted in the sanctified practice (Chapter 1, Fig. 4), was also prevalent as the style exercised by Charlie Patton, Son House, Willie Brown, Bukka White, and their imitators and contemporaries. In their improvised performances, the linear blues was a melody-based craft with the instrumental aspects of bass strumming and treble licks layered below and above it. To be sure, the treble licks were consonant with the bass tones, but rather than being vertically tied to each other with closed-interval chords, the treble and bass components could and usually did move independently. In short, the classic style is biphonic and birhythmic, if not polyphonic and polyrhythmic. The rare exception to this was Skip James, who pursued harmonic accentuation through his D minor "crossed note" tuning and technique in the blues.

Johnson's "Last Fair Deal Gone Down" shows him as a creative imitator of the "linear" polyphonic style of Patton and House. But he was not executing that style by rote. As we noted before, he could take "32–20 Blues" by Skip James, a song outside the classic practice, and rearrange it so well in the linear manner as to outdo the old masters with its throbbing, propulsive bass beat.

In the fifth chorus of "Last Fair Deal Gone Down" mentioned above (Fig. 13), he gives a jolt of dense closed interval chords. They seem inspired not by the controlled arrangements of Jubilee-style singing, but perhaps by the kinds of chords Johnson as a teenager could have played on a harmonica. Perhaps the reason why he had trouble learning the guitar was that he also had to adjust to the melodic-linear kind of playing, instead of the harmonic-vertical sort. Those "they count, they pick an' sing" chords may be Johnson coming full circle back to his cherished homophonic chords, and they hint at his future innovations in blues harmony.

New Horizons

In late 1932 or 1933, Johnson seemed to have moved to Helena, in the Arkansas Delta, but within easy traveling distance of the Mississippi Delta and Memphis. In a journeyman way, he had learned all he encountered about Delta blues guitar: he could play in standard and open-chord tunings, fret with or without a bottleneck slide, and could handle the bass, middle, and treble ranges of the guitar with equal ease and independence.

Charlie Patton, one of the guitarists Johnson regularly looked to for fresh ideas, was in failing health in 1933, and in April 1934 died in the Indianola-Holly Ridge area. Two months before his death, Patton and his wife went to New York for his last recording session. One of the pieces he did was "Oh Death," which he developed from the same melody as "You Gonna Need." By the time the news of Patton's death would have reached Helena, Johnson may no longer have been looking to him and other guitarists, but instead to pianists for new elements to add to his guitar improvisation, and for some ways of exercising his harmonic elements.

CHAPTER FOUR

Black River Blues: Blues Pianism 1930-1933

"Are These Tunings Correct?"

After three chapters of "possibly," "probably," and "may have," a few paragraphs of "did," "thought," and "definitely" are in order. For now, the 1930s will be left for 1996, when author Dave Rubin visited me at the University of Mississippi Blues Archive. While reading through the existing literature on Robert Johnson, we found most—if not all—of it had little to say for the years 1933 into 1935 other than his passing associations with other musicians and that he "rambled" all over the South. In fact, there was almost nothing available to explain the kind of advancement in harmonic thinking Johnson underwent in order to produce his recorded performances of "Kind Hearted Women Blues," "Sweet Home Chicago," and "Cross Road Blues." In addition, Dave wanted to know how Johnson combined boogie-bass figures with treble-string licks, but he wasn't finding the answer in standard or open tunings. The available transcription books on Johnson's music were of little use, as here and there the transcriptions were altered, apparently to fit in conventional guitar tunings. We weren't alone in our opinion. Jeff Jacobson, a Hal Leonard freelance transcriber, also wondered if the commonly attributed tunings were wrong.

When it came time to investigate the music discussed in this and the following chapters, Dave and I recognized that we had to isolate and identify the distinctive characteristics of Johnson's style in each song. Then, we would have to rethink the guitar tunings to fit those characteristics, rather than vice versa as had been others' previous efforts. Not everything we set for ourselves could be done within Dave's short stay at the Blues Archive, but the individual tasks we took on could be coordinated by phone and mail.

Searching for Precedents

I began my part of the work by searching through the Blues Archive for melodic precedents on records before 1936. I had to call such recorded appearances "precedents" rather than "sources," as there was no certain way to know if Johnson heard those melodies through individual records or from an imitator. Still, precedents could be useful as indicators of practices and innovations in blues musical trends in Johnson's time. I prepared myself for this task by transcribing Johnson's themes and thus committing them to memory. While doing this, I was reminded of his adoptions of the vocal mannerisms of Leroy Carr and Peetie Wheatstraw, so I first examined their records. At that time, the Blues Archive had just received the Document pre-war blues reissue series containing the complete recordings of Carr, Wheatstraw, and almost every other blues artist before 1942, except for Johnson, whose reissue was handled by Sony/Columbia. The Carr and Wheatstraw discs in that series yielded many indications from 1928 through 1935 of themes later picked up by Johnson. The discs of Roosevelt Sykes and his fellow St. Louis pianists helped to enlarge the number of additional relevant musical elements. When I felt I had a reasonably comprehensive accounting of Johnson's themes, I drew up a chart of findings and sent one copy to Dave and another to *Living Blues* for publication in the September 1996 issue.[78]

With that chart, I began listening in depth to the blues piano records, and in them I discerned the blues piano accompaniment trend of four chordal beats per measure in common time, from Leroy Carr's first records in 1928 to other pianists, including those in St. Louis. I felt that such a trend had to have been noticed by Robert Johnson in Mississippi, and after some comparison I came to believe that he successfully transcribed the then-contemporary piano accompaniments for guitar. Just when he may have done so wasn't exactly clear: few records by any artist were issued in 1932 and 1933, the worst years of the Depression, and the surviving published remembrances of Johnson didn't place him in St. Louis until 1935 or so.

[78] Komara 1996

The Mystery Tuning

Meanwhile in Manhattan, Dave began listening to the records listed on my report and through comparing them to Johnson's he was able to identify the bass runs, ornamental licks, passing chords, and introductions that Johnson added to each existing theme. The hardest and most important elements to be identified were the passing tones between tonic chords in the fills of "Cross Road Blues." Dave was not satisfied with the published efforts of previous transcribers, yet he felt that a truly faithful notated rendering of those moments was still possible. I shared his concern over those chords, for they were the most intriguing bits of Johnson's "Cross Road Blues" when I first heard it in 1983, and they fascinated me still. We knew those chords and their realization on the guitar were the keys to understanding Robert Johnson's music. For the better part of a week in October 1996, we hashed out all kinds of chords on guitar and piano, and finally we identified the "Cross Road" passing chords as I7 and vi:

Fig. 14 – Robert Johnson, "Cross Road Blues (Crossroads)"

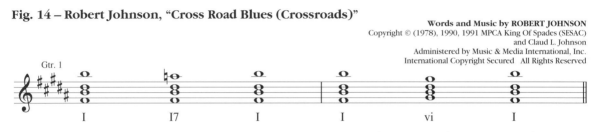

Dave then began figuring how Johnson's musical elements from piano blues fit together on the guitar. He didn't believe the standard and open tunings worked, even when the surviving members of the Robert Johnson generation, among them Johnny Shines and David "Honey Boy" Edwards, used them to play Johnson's songs. He also found the existing published transcriptions inadequate, since they directed the index and middle fingers of the fretting hand to be on the treble strings and the ring and pinky fingers to be stretched awkwardly to the bass strings. Granted, Johnson may have had long spidery fingers, but Dave believed that Johnson must have used a simple technique of index and middle fingers on the bass strings and ring and pinky on the treble. So, Dave began experimenting with alternate tunings, with the two top treble strings tuned a minor third apart, and the bass strings in an open chord. The unsuccessful early efforts throughout 1997 sounded as though he was trying to put two guitars together, and Johnson's use of open strings often ruled out these experimental tunings. Nothing seemed to work as a unified whole. "Johnson is kicking my butt," Dave once admitted. Finally, in February 1998, Dave, along with Hal Leonard guitar editors Jeff Schroedl and Jim Schustedt, found the solution in the Aadd9 tuning (E–B–E–A–C#–E), heretofore unknown to have been used by any other country blues guitarist. It was a technical breakthrough that led everyone involved to look at solo blues guitar in a whole new way.

Johnson, whenever he developed his technique on the Aadd9 tuning, apparently worked in isolation, and afterwards was reportedly protective of it. To this extent, he resembled the old Delta planters who guarded their lands and sharecroppers. In the absence of secondhand accounts, I have informed this chapter and the next with my and Dave's experiences from our research.

Returning to the 1930s: when did Johnson achieve his technical breakthrough of adapting piano elements for the guitar? His "Me and the Devil Blues" may be a clue. When first listening to his 1937 recording of it, I thought it was a slightly modified variant of his "Kind Hearted Woman Blues" recorded the previous year. In fact, "Kind Hearted Woman Blues" was based on Bumble Bee Slim's 1935 "Cruel Hearted Woman," which in turn was based on Leroy Carr's 1934 "Mean Mistreater Mama." Later, I found a 1929 record by Leroy Carr, "Prison Bound Blues," whose melodic opening matched that of "Me and the Devil Blues"; this kind of neighbor-tone opening hardly (if ever) occurs elsewhere in recorded pre-war blues.

Fig. 15A – Leroy Carr, "Prison Bound"

*downstemmed notes only, except during the turnarounds

From this I came to believe—and this is only a belief—that Johnson, long aware of the piano, successfully developed his Aadd9 technique to arrange piano blues for the guitar in or around 1933, when there were few if any records being released. Then, he quickly tested it against the first records widely available in 1934 and early 1935.

Robert Johnson, Harmonica Player

From the beginning, Johnson must have had an interest in the harmonic aspects of the blues. Remember—the mouth organ (harmonica), or "blues harp," was the first instrument he was known to have played. It is related to the push-button accordion, which was developed in the early nineteenth century and was common in Mississippi from after the Civil War through the 1910s. By Charlie Patton's time, the accordion was falling into disuse, although Walter Rhodes recorded a version of the "Banty Rooster" melody on that instrument for Columbia in 1928. It consisted of a set of reeds controlled by fingers on push buttons, and through the reeds a column of air would be pushed with bellows by the hands.[79] The harmonica is played on the same principle, except the player's lungs are the bellows and the reed sets are attached side to side to play the chosen tones. What the accordion and the harmonica had in common was this: to play a scale with the seventh tone flatted (Mixolydian mode), it had to be played from the fifth scale tone of the preset key (e.g. for an instrument in the key of D, start on A). Where they differed was portability and cost: the harmonica could be carried in a pocket and cost a few cents to buy.

Playing Blues on the Diatonic Harmonica

The diatonic harmonica consists of a set of reeds, each of which produce different tones when a player breathes in or out. When the reeds are blown from left to right, the D major harmonica (for example) produces a series of notes falling within a D major (tonic) triad, namely: D1–F#1–A1–D2–F#2–A2–D3–F#3–A3–D4. When drawn in, the successive tones are: E1–A1–C#2–E2–G2–B2–C#3–E3–G3–B3.

When combined (see Fig. 16, below), the blown and drawn tones for the middle four holes make up the D major scale, and are the basis for "straight harp" technique. Yet bluesmen like Johnson needed

Fig. 16 – Harmonica in D

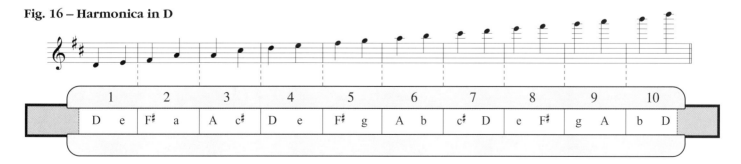

---

[79] Snyder 1997

that flatted seventh scale tone (C♮), which is not provided for on a D harmonica. But by drawing on the second hole of that D instrument, the player now begins the key of A, which has G at the fifth hole, the flatted seventh degree, hence second position (Mixolydian mode) or "cross harp" technique. Another way to approach the problem is to play a harmonica that is keyed a 4th (A to D, for instance) above the key of the song to obtain the flatted seventh. In the key of D, this would translate to a G harmonica to obtain the flatted seventh (C). An additional benefit of "cross harp" is the means to bend reeds by sucking air in, thus tailoring certain reeds to the preferred microtonal inflections favored by blues musicians, along with the flatted 3rd.

In addition, two other possibilities available to the blues harp player are the third position (Dorian mode) for the key of E minor, and the fourth position (Aeolian mode) for the key of B minor, both of which are also derived from the D harmonica. Johnson's great Mississippi Delta blues contemporary, Aleck "Sonny Boy Williamson II" Miller (who grew up in Tutwiler, MS in the mid-1920s), later became a superb blues harmonica technician in the third and fourth positions.[80] However, since the diatonic harmonica lacks some scale tones in the lower and upper ends of the reed set, it is not well suited for transposition (like the guitar and piano) into other keys.

The Role of the Piano in Johnson's Guitar Technique

As discussed in the previous chapter, pianos were not often found in the cluster communities of sharecroppers dotting the spacious Delta plantations. Yet apparently after receiving his first guitar, Johnson wished to play piano blues on it, as the remembrance of him playing Leroy Carr's "How Long How Long Blues" indicates. On the record, Carr plays in the key of E♭, and to replicate the bass figure on guitar Johnson would have needed the open bottom strings (see Chapter 3, Fig. 11B). Interestingly, on his records, Johnson was often tuned down a half step to E♭, capoing up when he needed to be in a higher key.

Hazlehurst jukes, supported by lumber and sawmill laborers, would have had upright pianos. Johnson may well have begun working with pianos during his year with Ike Zinnerman. With its layout of chromatic pitches, the piano enables the realization of different scales and the assembly of open- and close-voiced chords in various registers. Its hammers strike tones from the rack of strings, and the volume of those tones varies according to the pianist's force on the keys attached to the hammers.

Although the guitar is a plectrum instrument, its volume varies according to the player's touch on the strings themselves. Despite the fact that the pitch range of the guitar is less than three full octaves, it matches those of most singing voices and falls in the middle of the piano's pitch range (see Fig. 17). Therefore, with some ingenuity, a guitarist could be capable of simulating the piano's chordal accompaniment and lead solos at the same time, with separate gradations of loud and soft volumes (partially accomplished by muting) for each part.

Johnson may not have needed the piano to develop his technical innovations for guitar, but without it and its blues repertory he would have been in a less likely position to consider certain musical

Fig. 17 – Instrument Ranges

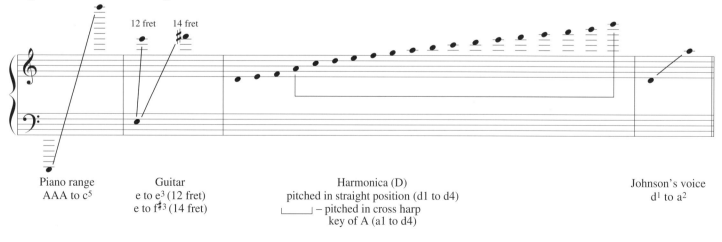

Piano range
AAA to c⁵

Guitar
e to e³ (12 fret)
e to f#³ (14 fret)

Harmonica (D)
pitched in straight position (d1 to d4)
└─────┘ – pitched in cross harp
key of A (a1 to d4)

Johnson's voice
d1 to a2

[80] Glover 1965, 49-51

elements in general, and to plot their positions on a guitar fretboard. As he developed the pianistic qualities in his guitar technique, his use of the harmonica apparently lessened until he didn't bother to play it during his recording sessions. Nevertheless, certain blues harp elements appear to have been retained and embedded in some of his most densely rendered performances.

Little Brother Montgomery and Other Blues Pianists in the South

Mississippi blues south of the Delta has had its fair share of pianists.[81] As early as the 1900s and 1910s, New Orleans keyboardists played their rags and blues throughout the Gulf Coast. In 1938, the renowned Jelly Roll Morton recalled for Alan Lomax performing (when not hustling pool) in McHenry, Hattiesburg, Jackson, Vicksburg, Greenwood, Greenville, Gulfport, and Biloxi.[82]

In 1930 a couple of Mississippi pianists made records. On that trip to Grafton with Charlie Patton and Son House, Louise Johnson made "On the Wall," a version of Cow Cow Davenport's pioneering 1925 boogie woogie classic "Cow Cow Blues," aptly replicating his boogie line of the IV chord:

Fig. 18 – Louise Johnson, "On the Wall"

By LOUISE JOHNSON

Louise Johnson also recorded "By the Moon and Stars," a rendering of "Vicksburg Blues" that was widely performed throughout Mississippi by Eurreal "Little Brother" Montgomery.[83]

Montgomery at that time was regarded as among the finest Deep South pianists, and around September 1930, he made his own authoritative recording of "Vicksburg Blues." With his nasal voice singing the melody, his piano accompaniment consists of triadic chords in the treble register and whole or half note tones in the bass (Fig. 19).

Although Montgomery's delivery of the theme was distinctive, the melody was copied by others, including Skip James, who in the piano section of his 1931 session adapted it for his "What Am I to Do

Fig. 19 – Eurreal, "Little Brother" Montgomery, "Vicksburg Blues"

---

[81] for a map of Mississippi blues piano towns, see Gert zur Heide 1970, 56-57
[82] Lomax 1950, 113
[83] Komara 1997a, 12, 28

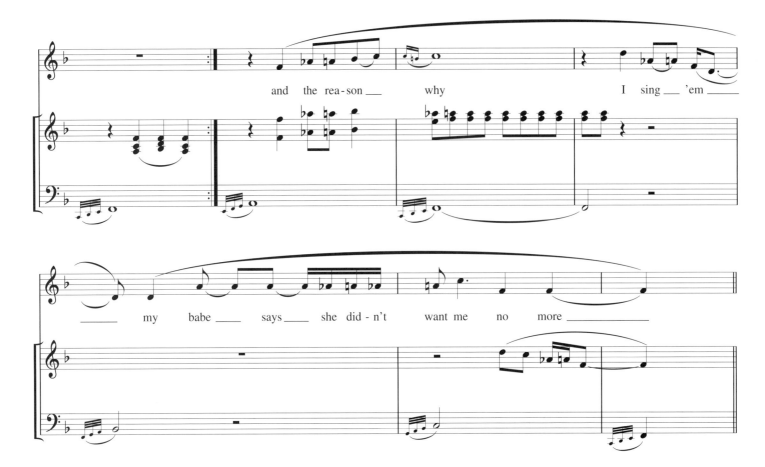

and the rea-son ___ why ___ I sing ___ 'em ___

___ my babe ___ says ___ she did - n't want me no more ___

Blues." A Hattiesburg pianist of this era was Cooney Vaughan, of whom Montgomery in later years spoke with admiration.[84] Another Mississippi pianist who shared Montgomery's piano practices was Lee Green, who titled his rendition of "Vicksburg Blues" as "Number 44 Blues" after the train running on the Yazoo and Mississippi Valley ("Yellow Dog") line of the Illinois Central railroad. He needed not the Yellow Dog, but another line of the Illuinois Central to reach Helena, Arkansas, where Roosevelt Sykes claimed to have first met him in 1925.

Roosevelt Sykes and the Blues of St. Louis

Sykes was prominent in St. Louis blues of the 1930s and brought many of his friends and musical associates in their performing primes to the recording studios. Born in 1906 in Elmar, Arkansas, he grew up in Helena, learning organ at first but then switching to piano. Upon learning the "44s" theme and style from Lee Green, he then moved in the late 1920s to St. Louis, from where he would travel to Memphis, Helena, and Chicago. In his version of the "44s," he retained the piano accompaniment but not the theme; he also changed the lyrical subject from trains to guns, presumably for his urban audiences. He and Green recorded their individual versions of the "44s" in 1929, much to Montgomery's later dismay ("…they beat me to Chicago and put them out.").[85]

St. Louis, long the "Gateway to the West," was in the 1920s and 1930s becoming the "Gateway to the North." With its industries, the city was attractive to blacks tired of the uncertainties of sharecropping and who sought better lives than what they had in the Jim Crow South. Those who had to live across the river in East St. Louis, Illinois, learned it was the site of a fierce race riot in 1917 that was still straining relations between blacks and whites.[86] Others who could not find a place in the area moved on to Chicago. Coming as they did from different southern states and regions, black audiences in St. Louis requested various kinds of blues. Sykes's first records in June 1929 are good indications of those tastes. In addition to "44 Blues," he performed the hokum "I'm Tired of Being Mistreated," a version of Pine Top Smith's "Pine Top's Boogie Woogie" of 1928 called "Boot That Thing," and two blues, "All My Money Gone"

[84] Gert zur Heide 1970, 32
[85] Oliver 1968, 102
[86] Oliver 1970, 90

and "The Way I Feel," sung in Lonnie Johnson's vocal style. The releases were successful enough to lead to additional sessions, and he would record under pseudonyms like Doby Bragg and Willie Kelly. However, his best known nickname, "The Honey Dripper," came from a blues title at an Edith North Johnson session in September 1929 that he accompanied.

If commercial recordings from 1927 through 1931 are any indications, many St. Louis singers were influenced by Lonnie Johnson (who was living in the city then), or at least they recognized his style as one in demand from the record labels. Two singers from 1927, Jelly Roll Anderson and Bert "Snake Root" Hatton, were accompanied by Lonnie Johnson himself on guitar. But other vocalists sang like him with pianos. Among them were Robert Peeples in 1929 on "Fat and Greasy Baby," and Specks McFadden, also in 1929 with Roosevelt Sykes, on "Misunderstood Blues" and "Don't Bite That Thing." Even women took up Johnson's style of delivery, such as Alice Moore who scored a hit with "Black and Evil Blues" in 1929.

The nature of the piano accompaniments seemed to vary according to the singer's talent and the quality of the material. When pianists like Sykes, Wesley Wallace, or Henry Brown (not to be confused with singer "Hi" Henry Brown) sang, they were likely to accompany themselves with a "44 Blues" style, a stepwise boogie bass, or the "stride" style of alternating two bass tones an octave or a tenth apart. However, if the lyrics had some conceptual or narrative quality, or the singer was of unknown or of modest ability, a subdued accompaniment of quarter-note bass chords (sometimes reinforced by a triplet eighth note before each beat; see Fig. 20) in 4/4 time would be used. For examples, one should listen to Henry Brown's piano behind Alice Moore's "Black and Evil," Sykes's on Specks McFadden's 1929 version of "Piggly Wiggly Blues," or Wesley Wallace's on Bessie Mae Smith's "St. Louis Daddy."

Fig. 20 – Quarter-note bass rhythms in piano blues

(1) basic   (2) with triplet reinforcement   (3) alternate notation of (2)

Leroy Carr

When performing live in a club or a crowded house rent party, many of these singers would have had to project above the din. On records, their voices sound a little ragged and worn from heavy use and lack of voice training. The first records of Leroy Carr in 1928 must have been popular not so much for his piano accompaniments, which differed little from those of Henry Brown or Wesley Wallace, but more likely for his suave crooning of the blues. His voice was seamless between the middle and high registers, enabling an easy delivery of blues melodies ascending at the last four measures of each chorus. His frequent habit of placing a high "ooh" in the middle lyric of each chorus became widely imitated. He was among the first blues singers to recognize the magnifying power of the electric recording microphone, and on his records he never rushed his tempo or forced his volume at the expense of his vocal smoothness.

Carr was born in 1905 in Indianapolis, Indiana. Although he learned piano at an early age, he seemed uninterested in playing it for virtuosity's sake. He was capable of a light "walking" boogie pattern as on "You Got to Reap What You Sow" (Fig. 21), but he usually kept his piano accompaniment in subdued, common time beats.

Figure 21 – Leroy Carr, "You Got to Reap What You Sow"

By LEROY CARR

In June 1928, Carr went to a Vocalion Records field recording unit visiting Indianapolis and performed his rendition of a 1925 Ida Cox record, "How Long Daddy How Long." Assisting him was guitarist Scrapper Blackwell, who picked treble licks during the fills and turnarounds between lyrics and choruses. The resulting "How Long How Long Blues" was such a hit that Vocalion retained them for sessions in Chicago. Their success continued with "Prison Bound Blues" (1928) and "Straight Alky Blues" (1929). Both sold very well upon release and were taken up by other musicians.

Roosevelt Sykes did one such borrowing by using Carr's "Straight Alky Blues" melody as the basis for "Black River Blues." Where Carr sang "I went down to Smith St., to buy some al-kee-hol," Sykes sang with a stride piano bass "I went down to the Black River, fell down on my knees." On his other records of this period, Sykes continued to vary his approach, from his common-time beats for Henry Townsend in 1929, to hokum such as "We Can Smell That Thing" (1930), and Lonnie Johnson-inflected vocals in 1931. He even did a bit of Mississippi blues in 1932, transforming Patton's "Banty Rooster Blues" theme into "Highway 61 Blues," possibly to appeal to his audiences in the Delta areas of Arkansas and Mississippi.

Walter Davis and Peetie Wheatstraw

In 1930, with the presence of Sykes at the piano, Walter Davis sang "M. & O. Blues" at his first session. The song was so popular that its melody was picked up by Sykes for his own sessions (such as "Mr. Sykes' Blues," 1932) and by Leroy Carr. In fact, the success of Davis's "M. & O. Blues" was so great that the singer remade it several times as an established Victor artist. Its title recognition was so taken for granted that, as Gayle Wardlow believes, several copies of Willie Brown's Delta blues of the same title were sold in error to customers who did not specify the artist to sales clerks.

Another singer who emerged in St. Louis at this time was William Bunch, better known as Peetie Wheatstraw, "the High Sheriff of Hell, the Devil's Son-In-Law." A musician who used the same theme on most of his records, Wheatstraw earned his success by boasting his lyrics in a coarse, carefree manner. Born in 1902 in Ripley, Tennessee, he came to St. Louis in the late 1920s. His main theme, starting with "So Long Blues" (1930), appears to be a variant of Carr's "Prison Bound Blues," with an abrupt melodic jump in the second measure (see Fig. 22, for its use in "Police Station Blues") and frequently opened vocally with "ooh, well well." His accompaniment was usually common-time chordal beats. Later in time, perhaps in 1933 or early 1934, he began using the same introduction to his recorded blues,[87] which for all its recurrence includes some harmonic touches like the minor vi chord.

Fig. 22 – Peetie Wheatstraw, "Police Station Blues"

St. Louis Guitarists

Oddly, guitarists in and around St. Louis at this time did not seem to be influenced much by the piano, or much interested in playing piano-based repertory. To be sure, guitarists could strum in common time, but unlike their piano-playing colleagues, they would break off from bass-string strumming to execute a treble string lick, like Scrapper Blackwell (on his solo discs without Leroy Carr), Henry Spaulding, and Henry Townsend. Charley Jordan, on "Stack O' Dollars Blues" (1930), maintained a thumbed-bass string to sound like a pianist except when reaching for a note far up the fretboard. The rest of his solo guitar accompaniments center on the treble strings with an occasional bass tone.

---

[87] Garon 1971, 31

J.D. Short evidently liked to play some fills on the bass strings (as on "Lonesome Swamp Rattlesnake," 1930). Teddy Darby preferred treble strings and, like Charley Jordan, he reserved his low strings for the occasional bass tone. With the exception of the Indianapolis-born Blackwell, Darby appears to be the only one among recorded St. Louis guitarists before 1934 to adopt a piano blues theme. This was Walter Davis's "M. & O. Blues," as the basis for "Low Mellow" in 1933, but he performed it in his accustomed guitar style. Even Peetie Wheatstraw, in his infrequent guitar sides, was content to merely strum down the strings, instead of imitating the piano.

Record Industry in Eclipse

From 1930 through 1933, the record industry was in a steep decline, following the general economy since the stock market crash of October 1929. Total records sold by the entire recording industry in 1921, the year of Mamie Smith's "Crazy Blues" success, were about 100 million, while the total sold in 1932 was a mere 6 million.[88] Some blues labels folded, including Paramount in 1932. Others were sold to larger companies, such as the American Recording Company to Consolidated Film Industries (CFI) in 1930, Brunswick and Vocalion to CFI in 1931, and Columbia/Okeh to Grisby-Grunow in 1931. Victor was purchased by the Radio Corporation of America (RCA) in 1929 and thus survived the Depression, but it halted its field recording sessions for the time being in 1932.

The remaining labels and their artists grimly held on through 1933, the year newly elected U.S. president Franklin Roosevelt enforced a bank holiday. Roosevelt Sykes recorded when he could for Victor and Champion, but the releases were issued in limited quantities. Leroy Carr fared worse; for all his popularity on records, he did not record for Vocalion or another label from March 1932 until February 1934. The supply of new records (blues and otherwise) was nearly stopped in 1933.

The musical trends brought by St. Louis bluesmen on records through 1933 were new and exciting. The ironic, if at times self-deprecating vocal style of Lonnie Johnson, was giving way to the suavity of Leroy Carr. Blues singers were more than ever being accompanied by pianists in chordal beats in steady 4/4 time. This kind of accompaniment was not polyrhythmic like the conventional Delta practice. Rather, it used homophonic chords whose tones sounded together in pulsing rhythms as opposed to separate melodies. Although simple intervals like fifths and octaves and the basic concepts in triadic harmony were retained, the harmonic ground was set for new kinds of chords like the minor vi chord in different inversions. New melodic themes were introduced, like Davis's "M. & O. Blues" and Carr's "Prison Bound Blues," that were best sung with urbane ease. Blues guitarists had yet to give an approximate transcription of the piano on their instruments, and those in St. Louis seemed unconcerned about doing so.

Yet Robert Johnson, by now living in Helena, Arkansas, must have already conceived and believed in the possibility of playing a current St. Louis piano accompaniment on one guitar. His focus on this musical goal may explain why he did not later record any guitar "stomps" or the James "Stump" Johnson brand of ribald blues then popular. How he followed the blues styles that intrigued him, whether through records or by seeing Arkansas-born bluesmen like Roosevelt Sykes when they were visiting family living near him, is not known. What is evident from the records he made in 1936 and 1937 is that he succeeded in playing piano accompaniments on a guitar, and the melodies he used on them are clues to his path to achievement.

---

[88] Dixon, Godrich and Rye, 1997, xiii

CHAPTER FIVE

Cross Road Blues: Johnson as Guitar Revolutionary

Robert Johnson probably did not conceive his piano-style technique all at once. More likely, he developed it by solving a series of technical problems with his acute harmonic sense. String by string, lick by lick, song by song, Johnson produced a body of blues in emulation of the top piano blues stars of the 1930s. The results include some of his most recognized and celebrated songs, especially "Dust My Broom," "Kind Hearted Woman Blues," "Ramblin' on My Mind," and most recognized by today's blues fans, "Sweet Home Chicago." On Johnson's 1936 recordings, these tunes are performed with ease and abandon. Yet a few years earlier, each of them must have presented individual technical challenges to him.

By Way of Introduction: Arthur Petties

St. Louis guitarists may have seemed uninterested in adapting piano licks, but in the late 1920s a Mississippi Delta guitarist recorded some attempts at doing so.

Arthur Petties (or Pettis) recorded in 1928 in Memphis and in 1930 in Chicago. In the 1950s and 1960s, older bluesmen remembered him being in Jackson[89] or Bolivar County in the Delta.[90] A later commentator, Stephen Calt,[91] places him in Tunica County. Petties later moved to Chicago. Whichever of these locations are correct, he would have been well within the sphere of Johnson's activity and travels for 1928 through 1934.

It is likely that Johnson heard Petties in person, if not on records. To begin his "Quarrelin' Mama Blues" (1930), Petties makes a melodic leap of a major 6th on his guitar to the third scale tone, then steps down to the tonic (F♯ to D♯, then to B):

Fig. 23A – Arthur Petties, "Quarreling Mama Blues"

Six years later on the first take of "Phonograph Blues," Johnson uses the same motivic germ for his own introduction. This motif is very unusual and may be unique to Petties since it is not heard in other recordings of Delta musicians of the time; Johnson must have heard him.

---

[89] Big Joe Williams cited in Evans 1968
[90] Big Bill Broonzy to Paul Oliver, cited in John Vanco 1993
[91] with John Miller, 1973

Fig. 23B – Robert Johnson, "Phonograph Blues"

Open A Tuning; Down 1/2 Step:
(low to high) E♭–A♭–E♭–A♭–C–E♭

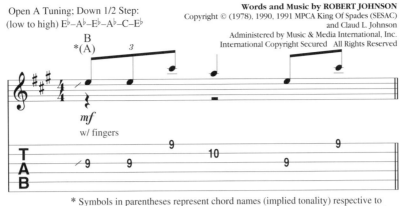

* Symbols in parentheses represent chord names (implied tonality) respective to
capoed guitar. Symbols above reflect implied tonality. Capoed fret is "0" in Tab.

One of the first piano-style problems Johnson had to solve was a chorus turnaround lick that began on the flatted 7th scale tone and descended by half steps to the 5th scale tone. This lick was used by blues pianists on records since the early 1920s (for example, Sara Martin's "Michigan Water Blues," 1923, with Clarence Williams on piano). Leroy Carr frequently used this turnaround lick on many of his 1928-1932 records, including the ones Johnson was certain to have studied. Petties's attempt to imitate this piano turnaround in chorus 7 of "That Won't Do" (see Fig. 24A) is marred by the cramped proximity of the treble and bass lines; the descending lower run seems to begin at the same D tone in the treble chord:

Fig. 24A – Arthur Petties, "That Won't Do"

Tune Down 1/2 Step:
(low to high) E♭–A♭–D♭–G♭–B♭–E♭

By ARTHUR PETTIES

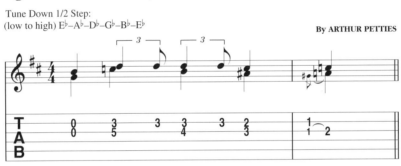

Johnson reset the descending run an octave lower, enabling a greater contrast between the treble and bass components, and producing a sound more in keeping with the piano model.

Fig. 24B – Robert Johnson, "Kind Hearted Woman Blues"

Tune Down 1/2 Step; Capo II:
(low to high) E♭–A♭–D♭–G♭–B♭–E♭

* Symbols in parentheses represent chord names (implied tonality) respective to capoed guitar.
Symbols above reflect implied tonality. Capoed fret is "0" in Tab.

It is strange that Petties's turnaround sounds muddled and unclear, for earlier in the same chorus he shows how to play a descending run an octave below the treble line:

Fig. 24C – Arthur Petties, "That Won't Do"

Tune Down 1/2 Step:
(low to high) E♭–A♭–D♭–G♭–B♭–E♭

By ARTHUR PETTIES

Also notable in this example are the repeated high notes in plucked triplets; this sort of playing is not heard in the records of other Delta masters like Charlie Patton, Son House, or Skip James. But Johnson uses these triplets as a recurring feature in most of his recorded introductions; the exceptions are those to "Ramblin' on My Mind," "Come On in My Kitchen," "Terraplane Blues," "They're Red Hot," and "Hell Hound on My Trail." But in the rest of his takes, the introductions may be heard as harmonically refined renderings of Petties's style of playing.

Piano Boogie Woogie and "R.L."

The piano's capability of performing boogie bass lines may have inspired Robert Johnson to try and imitate that quality on the guitar. His first effort might have been around 1932 in what may have been a two-guitar arrangement—one playing the boogie-bass pattern and the other providing treble licks and fills. He did not record such a piece, but in 1935 his Jackson colleague Johnny Temple did so in possibly the same way he had performed it with Johnson three years earlier.

The "Lead Pencil Blues" melody is similar to Son House's "My Black Mama." It is likely that Johnson supplied the theme, since Temple did not know House. The boogie bass figure may have also been a Johnson touch, since the pianists Temple knew, Little Brother Montgomery and Skip James, did not use such patterns in their styles. Moreover, although "Lead Pencil" was the first piece of his first recording session, Temple and his assisting guitarist Charlie McCoy did not employ boogie basses in the other blues recorded that day. The boogie bass in "Lead Pencil" is not scalar like those of Cow Cow Davenport or Leroy Carr, but rather close to those of Jabo Williams (see Figs. 25A and 25B). Williams was a pianist from Birmingham who also worked at times in St. Louis and recorded for Paramount in 1932. His bass patterns leap and dive during the offbeats between the stressed tonic note beats. It is uncertain whether Johnson and Temple heard Williams's records in Speir's store or whether they managed to see him perform in Birmingham, Hattiesburg, or Jackson. At any rate, the Jabo-esque bass pattern supports the year 1932 in Temple's recollection to Gayle Wardlow of having played with a musician named "R.L.," and Temple's application of the Son House style melody strengthens the interpretation that "R.L." was indeed Johnson.

Figure 25A – Jabo Williams, "Ko-Ko-Mo Blues" (meas. 5-8)

By Jabo Williams

Fig. 25B – Jabo Williams, "House Lady Blues" (meas. 1-4)

By Jabo Williams

Adapting Piano Techniques to the Solo Guitar

Johnson played alone most of the time and probably could not count on finding a reliable second guitarist wherever he went. To replicate (or at least come close to) piano sounds on one guitar, he had to change his understanding of both instruments.

As noted earlier (Chapter 4, Fig. 17), the guitar falls in the midrange of the piano, while the harmonica lays in the upper half of the piano's range. Johnson's voice, as reproduced on his records, appears to have had a tessitura from d1 to a2, which left him nearly an octave of guitar bass notes to work with.

What enables the piano's rich sound is the ability to provide overtones. A common demonstration is the production of the octave and fifth upon the silent depression of a bass key and the sharp striking of a treble key. Many guitarists today refer to these overtone phenomena as "sympathetic vibrations." Whether he called them overtones or vibrations, Johnson may have noticed them while trying out pianos in the early 1930s. He may have also noticed that each treble tone is fitted with a set of three strings. A guitar in standard tuning (E–A–D–G–B–E) is tuned in ascending 4ths, with the exception of the B string (3rd). So while the bass strings may produce a deep sound according to the quality of the guitar's construction, they may not vibrate much with the other strings according to the overtone series. By tuning the lowest string one whole step down to D, for example, you have the drop-D tuning (D–A–D–G–B–E) like Lonnie Johnson favored. It enables some, if not much, overtone vibration among the lower three strings due to the low octave note (D) and the full-sounding interval of a perfect 5th (D to A).

Cross Harp and Open A Tuning

On first appearance, the open A tuning (E–A–E–A–C♯–E) seems to be based on 4ths (paired E–A and E–A in the key of E). Country blues guitarists, however, saw it as a way to have an A major triad when all the open strings are strummed. But let it be remembered that Johnson began as a harmonica player. The D harmonica, when breathed out in "straight" technique, can produce in succession a series of D major triad tones. But the "cross" technique of drawing in the breath through the first four holes produces in succession the pitches E1–A2–C♯3–E4, the same ones to which the top four guitar strings are set in open A tuning. Breathing in through a single harmonica reed does not produce overtones among the other reeds in the instrument, although a sharp draw through the first and second holes (which are an interval of a fourth apart) produces a rich sound nonetheless. However, as noted earlier, the diatonic harmonica is not a transposing instrument, while a guitarist can change keys simply by placing a capo over the desired fret or by barring. In addition, the guitarist can imitate the harmonicist's drawn "bent" notes by bending the guitar strings. Johnson's full realization of the A major tuning as a harmonica-style setting will be discussed in the next chapter.

Open E Minor Tuning

After learning Skip James's blues from Johnny Temple, Johnson should have been familiar with the open D minor tuning (D–A–D–F–A–D). As previously mentioned, he did play "Hell Hound on My Trail" in open E minor tuning (E–B–E–G–B–E)—one whole step up from open D minor. This tuning is especially resonant with its two octave tones to the bottom strings and its two perfect fifths. Also, when the three E strings are sharply plucked at once, they produce a sound similar to the set of three strings for a treble piano tone.

While trying to figure a way to combine the resonance of the overtones, the tone layout of the harmonica, and the ability to play boogie bass lines and treble licks from piano blues records, Johnson must have tried all kinds of tunings and alternate means of fingering. Highly important in fingering would be the use of the index and middle fingers on the bass strings and as barre fingers on the treble ones.

The Mystery Tuning

Apparently, Johnson eventually discovered a solution to this dilemma within the Aadd9 tuning (E-B-E-A-C#-E). Though only one string away from open A (E-A-E-A-C#-E), it placed the tonic on string 6, making it function much differently from open A, or any other tuning for that matter. To the best of my knowledge and other experts in the field, this tuning is unique to Robert Johnson. To change back from Aadd9 to open A (his most used tuning), he only had to retune the fifth string (the B to A); he was then ready to play either his slide tunes with his bottleneck or additional piano tunes with his Aadd9 fretting technique modified.

The Aadd9 tuning could be discussed here as a derivative of the open A tuning. But I will refer to Aadd9 as a base tuning for the fingerplucking technique that Johnson used for his piano-based repertory, and to lessen the confusion with the open A tuning's other function as a setting for his harmonica-based repertory (to be discussed next chapter).

By formulating the Aadd9 tuning, Johnson elegantly codified an interrelated group of tunings to which he could perform many types of material. However, on his 1936 recordings, he seems to have the habit of tuning down his strings, then using a capo on the first or second fret. Each string of the twelve-fret guitar is capable of an octave before the neck joins the body. Therefore, if he was playing with a capo on the second fret, his execution of the upper octave licks would be greatly hampered. The thirteenth and fourteenth frets would be up over the body of a guitar (like the Gibson L1 that Johnson appears with in the studio photo) with no cutaway. Fortunately, fourteen-fret necks were introduced on Martin guitars in 1929 and were available on Gibson makes by 1932. Johnson made sure to get a fourteen-fret guitar before his first sessions in San Antonio.[92] He then could have a full octave string range (see Fig. 26) when he put his capo on the second fret, as can be seen in that cherished blues icon, the dime-store photograph of Johnson with cigarette. Interestingly, in conventional open and standard tunings, the chord Johnson frets makes no sense. But in the Aadd9 tuning, it is an F-based chord, to be used as a passing device between two strong chords.

Robert Johnson photo booth self portrait/early 1930s.

Fig. 26 – Guitar tunings and respective string ranges on a 14-fret guitar

Early Efforts and Stationary Basses

The most elementary boogie bass is the tonic stationary bass in repeated quarter notes in 4/4 time. Johnson used this to noticeable effect on his "Come On in My Kitchen" and "Me and the Devil Blues." To play this on the guitar, Johnson simply had to thumb on the fifth string—a simple enough technique.

In addition to the vocal opening noted earlier, another cause for wondering whether "Me and the Devil" was an early effort in adapting piano blues is the crude manner in which the Petties type of cho-

---

[92] See Rubin 2000B, 6-7 for a further discussion of this issue.

rus turnaround is attached. In the first beat of the turnaround measure, there is only a quarter rest of silence, with no bass pulse carried over from the previous measure. I can hardly believe my ears that Johnson played it this way on his 1937 recordings, in view of the refined versions of the turnaround he did for "Kind Hearted Woman Blues" and "I Believe I'll Dust My Broom." One possible reason is that he had not performed "Me and the Devil" for a few years, and he decided to leave the guitar accompaniment as it was, crudities and all.

There is also a slight likelihood that "Cross Road Blues" may have been first developed at this early time, given its strong melodic and lyric similarity to Roosevelt Sykes's "Black River Blues" (1930) and Leroy Carr's "Straight Alky Blues" (1929). If so, it was probably given a simple quarter note accompaniment on the open fifth and fourth strings, instead of the dense chord style used on the record in 1936.

Fig. 27 – Robert Johnson's "Cross Road," as it could have sounded in his piano style

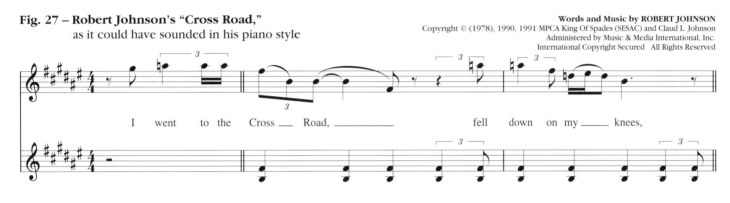

I went to the Cross ___ Road, _____ fell down on my ___ knees,

"I Believe I'll Dust My Broom"

"I Believe I'll Dust My Broom" was a song that may well have been developed by Johnson as early as 1933. Two recorded versions of the melodic theme had appeared by then; one was by the Sparks brothers, Aaron and Milton, as "I Believe I'll Make a Change" for Victor in 1932, and the other was by Jack Kelly and "His South Memphis Jug Band" as "Believe I'll Go Back Home" in 1933. Although Johnson may well have heard Kelly when visiting his Spencer siblings in Memphis, it is clear from his 1936 recording that he would have preferred the Sparks Brothers' piano and vocal arrangement. Although born twins in Tupelo, MS, the brothers were brought up in St. Louis, and their musical style on "I Believe I'll Make a Change" was steeped in the city's then-current blues trends.

Johnson decided to try an alternating "rocking" boogie pattern on this blues instead of a repeated monotone. To facilitate the fingering of the boogie on the fifth and sixth scale degrees, he apparently retuned the fifth string of the open A tuning from A to B, thus changing the tuning to Aadd9. The blazing, high dominant-tone lick at B below high C (at the tenth fret) is made possible by the C# and E strings of the Aadd9 tuning. Not to be missed, however, are the lightly touched ornamental figures during Johnson's vocal passages. In the chorus turnarounds, the Petties ending is used, but with the maintenance of the bass pulse to ease its entry on the second beat of that measure. In some of the turnarounds, he uses full triads and inverted chords; these may be later additions after his harmonic innovations with "Terraplane Blues." However, even with only its "rocking" boogie bass, Johnson's "I Believe I'll Dust My Broom" is a faithful transcription of big city blues piano and singing.

"Ramblin' on My Mind" and "When You Got a Good Friend"

Another blues theme that Johnson may have begun using at this time was "M. & O. Blues" popularized by Walter Davis and Roosevelt Sykes. He apparently heard this tune several different ways, for in 1936, he presented two accompaniments.

"Ramblin' on My Mind" is in the key of E and uses the same type of "rocking" boogie bass as in "Dust My Broom," hence it needs the two lowest strings set to E and B. He could use the Aadd9 tuning, but since he wants to pick some bottleneck-fretted licks, he would need to set the treble strings to the E-chord tones of G#-B-E, instead of the A-chord tones A-C#-E. The resulting tuning has to be in open E (E-B-E-G#-B-E), but with similar bass fingerings as to Aadd9. Aside from the rustic sounding

"Come On in My Kitchen," the two takes of "Ramblin' on My Mind" are the only ones among Johnson's performances to combine a boogie bass with bottleneck slide.

The other "M. & O."-style blues is "When You Got a Good Friend," also in the key of E. However, this piece contains a three-tone "walking" boogie bass in the manner of Leroy Carr's "You Gotta Reap What You Sow" (1929; see Chapter 24, Fig. 21). Johnson has to execute this scalar boogie from the fifth or dominant tone of the chord he happens to be using at the moment. This means during the first lyric phrase (when the chord is E), he has to start the pattern on the tone B; in the second phrase (when the chord is A), he has start on the tone E. To best ensure the consistency of the boogie, Johnson has to reset the strings so the fingerings of the scalar runs can take place on the same frets. He reset the fifth string to A and the fourth string to D. That way, he could begin the scalar boogie from the tone B on the second fret of the fifth string (I chord) and from the tone E on the second fret of the fourth string (IV chord).

With the adjustment of the fifth and fourth strings to A and D, it is obvious that open E will not be the tuning for "Good Friend" as it was for its sister tune "Rambling," but more similar to "Sweet Home Chicago" in standard tuning. The outer E strings will be retained, since they will be needed for the ground bass and the ornamental tones. He could leave the third string at G♯, but he retunes it to G♮ (or its enharmonic equivalent, F✕) to use as a leading tone to G♯ on some treble licks. Therefore, the tuning will be in standard E in accordance to the demands of the scalar "walking" boogie bass and the leading tone to G♯.

The Record Industry Recovers

Beginning in 1934, the record industry slowly rebuilt itself after the lean years of '32 and '33. The American Recording Company/Brunswick conglomeration purchased Columbia/Okeh and revived Vocalion. Victor began its Bluebird subsidiary for budget-priced records in 1933 and the next year it held its first commercial field session in two years recording, among others, Bo Carter and the Mississippi Sheiks in San Antonio. A new label emerged in the market, Decca, which began a 7000 series for black talent. It also bought the Champion trademark in 1935, on which Paramount performances by Willie Brown and Skip James were reissued.[93]

As new records by established stars emerged, it was interesting to see who survived the economic blackout. Two of Columbia's biggest names in blues and sacred music, Bessie Smith and Blind Willie Johnson, did not. Lonnie Johnson, so influential in St. Louis in the late 1920s, would not have another recording session until 1937.

Peetie Wheatstraw, Roosevelt Sykes, and Leroy Carr quickly reasserted themselves on records, although now with some musical interdependence. During the fallow period, they may have listened to each other's records for hit material to copy when they could record again. Thus Sykes, recording for the new Decca label, led off his first session of 1934 with "D.B.A. Blues," a Peetie Wheatstraw style tune. Carr, in his first session in two years, recorded "My Woman's Gone Wrong," based on Sykes's 1933 "I Done You Wrong," which in turn is a version of Davis's "M. & O. Blues". He also recorded a new melody with two separate sets of lyrics: "Mean Mistreater Mama" and "Blues Before Sunrise." Both became hits upon release.

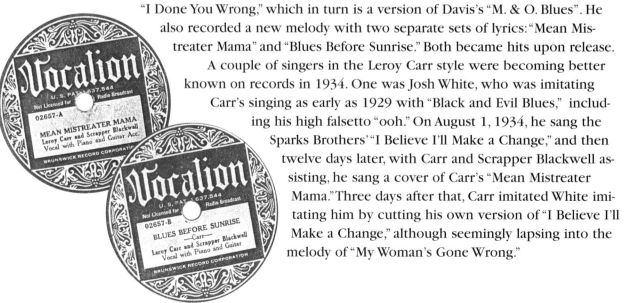

A couple of singers in the Leroy Carr style were becoming better known on records in 1934. One was Josh White, who was imitating Carr's singing as early as 1929 with "Black and Evil Blues," including his high falsetto "ooh." On August 1, 1934, he sang the Sparks Brothers' "I Believe I'll Make a Change," and then twelve days later, with Carr and Scrapper Blackwell assisting, he sang a cover of Carr's "Mean Mistreater Mama." Three days after that, Carr imitated White imitating him by cutting his own version of "I Believe I'll Make a Change," although seemingly lapsing into the melody of "My Woman's Gone Wrong."

---

[93] Dixon, Godrich, and Rye 1997, xxiv-xxxviii

Another guitarist who sang like Leroy Carr was Amos Easton, a.k.a. Bumble Bee Slim. Among his first records in 1931 was "Chain Gang Blues," a reworking of Carr's "Prison Bound Blues." The following year, he did a thinly disguised version of Davis's "M. & O. Blues" as "B. & O. Blues." But in September 1934, Easton added substitute lyrics to Carr's "Mean Mistreater Mama" to make "Cruel Hearted Woman;" and the next day, he did a straight version as "New Mean Mistreater Blues." But for all his imitation of Carr's musical style, Easton did introduce a new element: he started a new chorus with a contrasting secondary theme in eighth notes for the first four measures, then resumed with the established melody. He used this device to effect on "Climbing on Top of the Hill" and "Cold Blooded Murder," the latter another treatment of the "Mean Mistreater Mama" theme.

In October 1934, Walter Roland did a Leroy Carr piano-style cover of "Cold Blooded Murder," with guest guitarist Josh White filling in with some Scrapper Blackwell-style licks. Roland was a Birmingham musician who knew Jabo Williams's piano boogies like "Fat Mama" (or "Big Mama" as Roland's cover was titled on record) and "House Lady Blues" and was also a capable guitarist who could play two-guitar stomps with Sonny Scott.

From 1933 through 1935, Roland was best known as Lucille Bogan's piano accompanist on her best-selling blues records for A.R.C. Bogan was from Birmingham as well, but was a veteran of recording sessions from 1923 to 1930, when she did "Black Angel Blues," a herald of "Sweet Black Angel" later covered by Robert Nighthawk and B.B. King. Her first session with Roland in 1933 included the hit "Red Cross Blues," and in the following studio date they performed a popular cover of Specks McFadden's "Groceries on the Shelf." On these sides and others, Roland played the chordal common-time style in deference to the featured Bogan, yet he did play a good boogie for her on "House Top Blues."

While listening to these records on their initial release in 1934 and 1935, Johnson must have realized that the piano-style accompaniment he developed for guitar was more than special—it was unique! On their respective guitar performances, Josh White and Amos Easton were not capable of playing treble licks without abandoning the thumbed bass. Walter Roland, when playing solo guitar (as on "Red Cross Blues no. 2," 1933), kept to a heavy bass strum in common time with no treble ornamental licks.

"Come On in My Kitchen," "Me and the Devil Blues," "Kind Hearted Woman Blues," and "Little Queen of Spades"

Johnson capitalized on his guitar advantage by further developing its piano aspects. He added new licks from piano records, such as the turnaround figure from St. Louis Jimmy Oden's "Six Feet in the Ground" (1934; most likely played by Roosevelt Sykes) to "Come On in My Kitchen." It is interesting to note that "Six Feet," like "Kitchen," is based on the Sheiks' "Sitting on Top of the World."

Fig. 28 – Jimmy Oden, "Six Feet in the Ground" (1934), turnaround piano break
and Robert Johnson, "Come On in My Kitchen" (1936), turnaround guitar break

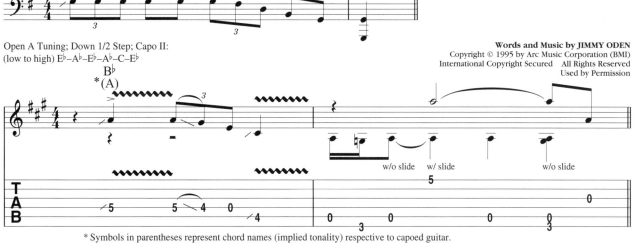

Open A Tuning; Down 1/2 Step; Capo II:
(low to high) E♭–A♭–E♭–A♭–C–E♭

* Symbols in parentheses represent chord names (implied tonality) respective to capoed guitar.
Symbols above reflect implied tonality. Capoed fret is "0" in Tab.

"Me and the Devil Blues" may have received some additions at this time as well. To the opening chorus of "Me and the Devil Blues," Johnson adopted Sykes's chiming chords from Walter Davis's "Night Creepin' "(see Fig. 29A). For the next chorus (see Fig. 29B), he borrowed Leroy Carr's secondary theme from "Blues Before Sunrise."

Fig. 29A – Robert Johnson, "Me and the Devil Blues"

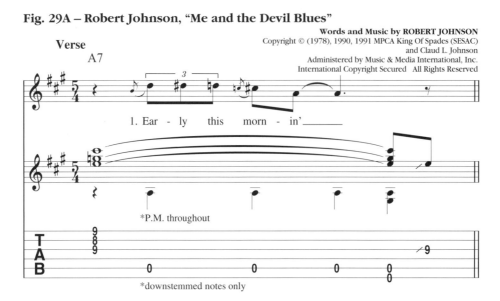

Fig. 29B – Robert Johnson, "Me and the Devil Blues," secondary theme

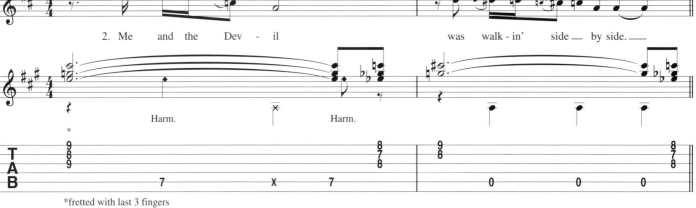

The guitar accompaniment for "Me and the Devil Blues" could have been the basis of "Kind Hearted Woman Blues," and the stylistic setting may have been chosen in part due to the melodic similarities of Leroy Carr's "Prison Bound Blues," "Mean Mistreater Mama" (1934), and Bumble Bee Slim's "Cruel Hearted Woman" (1934). Johnson retains the refined form of the Petties chorus turnaround as used in "Dust My Broom." To the primary theme, he added the secondary melody from Carr's "Blues Before Sunrise." And for a tertiary theme, he uses Bumble Bee Slim's contrasting device from "Cruel Hearted Woman,"; it should be noted that Johnson's singing of it resembles strongly the third chorus of Kokomo Arnold's "Milk Cow Blues," (which in turn was recorded on the same day (September 10, 1934) and at the same location (Decca label recording session, Chicago) as Easton's "Climbing on Top of the Hill" (Wald 2004, 134). On his recordings of this piece, Johnson sharply plucks the B7 and B°7 chords during the third chorus as bold homophonic strokes. Until this point, "Kind Hearted Woman Blues" could be listened to in linear polyphonic fashion. But those B7 and B°7 chords forces one to listen in a vertical manner, if only during that passage.

The same accompaniment was adapted yet again, this time to a different tune. In 1935, Peetie Wheatstraw recorded his signature theme "King of Spades," to which Johnson developed "distaff" lyrics as "Little Queen of Spades." These new words were applied to the Wheatstraw melody, which in turn was placed in the "Me and the Devil Blues"/"Kind Hearted Woman Blues"-style accompaniment.

"Sweet Home Chicago"

It must have been a serious musical challenge for Johnson to develop "Sweet Home Chicago." The melody on which the lyrics are set had long been used on records since at least 1926 (see Fig. 30). If the carefree manner in which Freddie Spruell sings it as a secondary theme in the last chorus of (1) is any indication, the melody may well have been sung to various sets of words for some time before 1926. Whatever its origins, the theme is used in its own right by Blind Blake in March 1927 (2) titled "One Time Blues." The following year, Arthur Petties, the guitarist Johnson likely heard in the Delta at the turn of the 1930s, recorded his own cover version as "Two Time Blues," with Blake-style double-timed guitar breaks between lyrics.

Figure 30 – Melodic Precedents (1926-1936) for Robert Johnson's "Sweet Home Chicago"

(1)	Freddie Spruell – Milk Cow Blues (last chorus only)	June 25, 1926
(2)	Blind Blake – One Time Blues	March 1927
(3)	Madlyn Davis – Kokola Blues	November 1927
(4)	Arthur Petties – Two Time Blues	February 14, 1928
(5)	Scrapper Blackwell – Kokomo Blues	June 16, 1928
(6)	Edith North Johnson – Honey Dripper Blues	September 7, 1929
(7)	Edith North Johnson – Honey Dripper Blues no. 2*	October 1929
(8)	Walter Fennel – Kokomo Blues *(unissued)	June 1930
(9)	Jabo Williams – Kokomo Blues	May 1932
(10)	Lucille Bogan – Red Cross Man	July 17, 1933
(11)	Walter Roland – Red Cross Blues	July 17, 1933
(12)	Walter Roland – Red Cross Blues no. 2	July 17, 1933
(13)	Sonny Scott – Red Cross Blues	July 18, 1933
(14)	Lucille Bogan – Kokomo Blues *(unissued)	July 19, 1933
(15)	Sonny Scott – Red Cross Blues no. 2	July 20, 1933
(16)	Isabel Sykes – In Here with your Heavy Stuff	August 2, 1933
(17)	Blind Willie McTell – Savannah Mama	September 18, 1933
(18)	Roosevelt Sykes – Big Legs Ida Blues	December 11, 1933
(19)	Charlie McCoy – Baltimore Blues	August 16, 1934
(20)	Kokomo Arnold – Original Old Kokomo Blues	September 10, 1934
(21)	Freddie Spruell – Mr. Freddie's Kokomo Blues	April 12, 1935
(22)	Georgia White – Honey Dripper Blues	July 15, 1935
(23)	Roosevelt Sykes – The Honey Dripper	February 21, 1936
(24)	Sam Montgomery – Where the Sweet Old Oranges Grow (unissued)	April 8, 1936
(25)	Sam Montgomery – The Honey Dripper*	April 11, 1936
(26)	Robert Johnson – Sweet Home Chicago	November 23, 1936

Note: Jack Kelly's "Ko-Ko-Mo Blues," recorded August 1, 1933 is not a precedent for "Sweet Home Chicago."
*unverified

As the table in Fig. 30 shows, the melody was used in at least one blues record a year from 1926 through Johnson's recording of "Sweet Home Chicago" in 1936, except for 1931 when very few blues records of any sort were being made. Early on, it was used in a series of songs about Kokomo ("That 'leven light city"), starting with a version by Madlyn Davis in 1927 (3, as "Kokola Blues"), then with Scrapper Blackwell's 1928 minor-mode inflected treatment (5). Jabo Williams made a classic piano boogie recording in two three-minute parts in 1932 (9), with the angular offbeat boogie patterns noted earlier as having an impact on Johnson and Johnnie Temple; he also introduces the device of numerical sums in the lyrics. Two intriguing possibilities by Walter Fennel (8) and Lucille Bogan (10) were unissued and may now be considered lost. As the record industry was lifting itself out of its economic doldrums, Charlie McCoy, who had assisted Johnny Temple on "Lead Pencil Blues," did a version where he substitutes Baltimore for Kokomo (19). Kokomo Arnold's famous 1934 "Original Old Kokomo Blues"(20) continues the "one and one is two, two and two is four" lyric component introduced by Jabo Williams. Apparently, Arnold's version was the lyrical model for "Mr. Freddie's Kokomo Blues" (21), with Spruell singing the same melody that he had unwittingly sung (1) nine years before.

Meanwhile, Edith North Johnson in 1929 sang the melody to another set of lyrics about her "Honey Dripper" (6 and 7). The pianist behind her was Roosevelt Sykes, who adapted the tune as the melodic basis for "In Here with Your Heavy Stuff" (16, sung by Isabel Sykes), "Big Legs Ida" (18), and his own reworking of "The Honey Dripper" (23). Georgia White's 1935 "Honey Dripper Blues" (22), with its minor-mode cast, may indicate her familiarity with Blackwell's "Kokomo" (5).

Although Lucille Bogan's version of "Kokomo Blues" (14) is unissued, we have some idea of how she sounded with that theme in "Red Cross Man" (10). She, Walter Roland, and Sonny Scott had traveled from Birmingham, Alabama to New York City for a marathon session for A.R.C. in July 1933. Between them were recorded six renditions of the melody (10–15, and likely the unissued 14) with five containing lyrics about the Red Cross stores distributing surplus food during the Depression. Bogan and Roland's respective versions became big hits. Years later, the family of Alabama blues musician Marshall Owens told Don Kent[94] that Roland stole "Red Cross Blues" from Marshall. The claim should be weighed in part in the context of the melody's use at this time, unless only the lyrics were referred to. It should also be noted that 10–15 are different from Walter Davis's "Red Cross Blues," which was recorded a month later to a Peetie Wheatstraw "Police Station Blues"-style melody.

There is no question that the "One Time"/"Kokomo"/"Red Cross" melody was popular in the South and St. Louis. Its appeal carried over to the Carolina Piedmont, where Blind Boy Fuller would use it as the basis for "Painful Hearted Man" and "Meat Shakin' Woman" in 1938.

Johnson's "Sweet Home Chicago" (26) is modeled after Williams' and Arnold's lyric arrangement in (9) and (20), but it is set in the piano styles of Sykes and Roland. Working in standard tuning, Johnson ably succeeded in executing the "walking" pattern noted for "When You Got a Good Friend." He also retains the high chordal lick on the G♮ and B pitches from "When You Got a Good Friend," in order to underscore the words "sweet home" at the end of every chorus. What's interesting about that passage is that the G♮ renders the tonality as A7, but the added B tone makes it become A9. Could this be an indication of the prevalence of the Aadd9 tuning in Johnson's mind, even in songs played in standard tuning like "Sweet Home Chicago" and "When You Got a Good Friend"?

Exactly what Johnson had in mind in singing about Chicago is difficult to say since St. Louis and Birmingham musicians used the melody more. Chicago bluesmen like "Big Bill" Broonzy and Tampa Red were not interested in this theme, and Johnson, in his time, would have been better received by singing "Sweet Home St. Louis." Perhaps he heard from others that St. Louis was becoming saturated with black labor and Chicago was the next "Promised Land." Sooner or later, Johnson would have to see St. Louis and Chicago for himself, and maybe even perform there. What may have been his most effective calling cards when he did go to those cities were shellac records with his name printed on the labels.

---

[94] Kent 1976, 7

CHAPTER SIX

Posterity and Destiny at the Crossroad

Lovers and Friends

While adapting big city piano blues to his guitar, Johnson certainly did not stay in one place. Helena's Hole in the Wall club was a good central base where he was remembered to have frequently played between 1932 and 1936.[95] However, he would have also continued making his rounds in the Mississippi Delta and the Jackson-Hattiesburg region and may have gone to St. Louis for the first time as early as 1933 or 1934.

While living in Hazlehurst, in 1931 Johnson remarried, this time to Caletta Craft. Unfortunately, their union eroded by the end of 1933, mostly due to his wife's illnesses from traveling with him.[96] He never married again, but instead took a number of lovers in the various towns he performed.

In Marvell, Arkansas, about 20 miles west of Helena on Highway 49, he frequently stayed with Estella Coleman, who in 1915 had bore a son to a man named Lockwood. When Johnson met her, her son Robert Lockwood was in his teens and already was playing guitar locally. Nevertheless, Lockwood learned what he could from Johnson. One wonders about the relationship between the two young men at the time. Lockwood would later be billed as Robert Jr. Lockwood in apparent reference to Johnson being a "stepfather." But Robert and Robert Jr. were only four years apart in age.

Johnny Shines

Perhaps in view of his piano-based repertory and guitar style, Johnson may have tended to associate with piano players while in Helena. It was through a regional pianist, Jerry "M. & O." Hooks that he met Johnny Shines, a young guitarist with a powerful voice then living in Hughes, Arkansas.[97] Up until then, Shines had idolized Chester "Howlin' Wolf" Burnett—who in turn had been inspired by Charlie Patton—to the extent that he thought the "Wolf" had sold his soul to the Devil to perform the way he did.[98] But when he heard Johnson for the first time, Shines thought he was in the presence of the greatest guitar player he had ever heard, being especially impressed by the bottleneck slide pieces.[99] From that time on, Shines traveled with Johnson whenever he could.

Harp Blues on Highway 61

One story Shines remembered in his later years was told as a testament to Johnson's showmanship, no matter the instrument. Both men had lost their guitars in a fire at John Hunt's hotel in West Memphis. Undeterred by their loss of instruments, Johnson and Shines headed north on Highway 61 towards Missouri. At a convenient spot on the highway side, Johnson produced a harmonica and began "patting his hands—blowing and singing," getting attention and tips from passing motorists. Shines was astonished by this display as he never knew until then that his companion was a great harmonica player, and he grew even more amazed when the change collected was enough to buy replacement guitars.[100] When they reached Steele, Missouri, they did buy new instruments, among them perhaps the fourteen-fret model that Johnson poses with in the dime-store photograph.[101] When Johnson bought a new guitar at this time, he apparently felt that fourteen frets were necessary for his technical needs.

---

95 Calt and Wardlow 1989, 46
96 LaVere, 11-13
97 Shines 1975, 26-27
98 Earl 1973, 10
99 Shines 1975, 27
100 Shines 1975, 28
101 Obrecht 1990a, 27

A New "Harmonica" Style of Accompaniment

Yet a fresh style of guitar playing may have resulted from this occurrence. Shines admitted that he never heard Johnson sing some of those harmonica songs before that day on Highway 61, but afterwards heard him replaying them on the guitar.[102] Perhaps the incident led Johnson to revive the harmonica style of accompaniment, this time on his guitar. He replaced the common-time piano-style bass pulse with ornamental bass beats and imitated the sharp draw of the cross-harp technique by sharply plucking the strings instead of strumming them down and up. Also important were the choice of chords and their inversions. Two that figure prominently in this style are I7 and vi, which are easily playable on the harmonica.

Fig. 31A – Robert Johnson, "Cross Road Blues (Crossroads)"
fill chords for guitar in tablature

Open A Tuning; Down 1/2 Step; Capo II:
(low to high) E♭–A♭–E♭–A♭–C–E♭

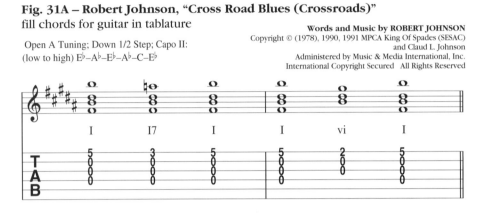

Fig. 31B – Robert Johnson, "Cross Road Blues (Crossroads)"
fill chords for harmonica in E diatonic

Exemplary in this "harp" style is Johnson's 1936 recording "Terraplane Blues." Its melody is that of Peetie Wheatstraw's "Police Station Blues," but it discards the strummed guitar accompaniment, as well as the common time piano used by Wheatstraw in his other recorded treatments of the theme. Instead, Johnson repeats a one-measure lick on the treble strings and reserves the bass strings for ornamental percussive beats that are reinforced by finger taps on the body of the guitar. The harmonica-like passages occur in the fills following each lyric, in which among regular tonic chords (A–C#–E–A) are open, inverted tonic 7ths (E–E–G–A) and closed minor vi chords in first inversion (A–C#–F#). For the V chord, he uses a brief form of Patton's "Screamin' and Hollerin'" dominant chord lick (see Chapter 2, Fig. 7B), then closes each chorus with more harmonica-type passages. Johnson may have not recorded with his harmonica, but his "Terraplane Blues" and others derived from it give a fair suggestion of his musicianship on that instrument.

The harmonica (or "harp") style uses homophonic chords towards accentuating harmonic aspects of the blues chorus structure. There is now a "vertical" manner of blues improvisation possible, although there is the risk of the blues chorus becoming disfigured by ill-chosen chords. Such a risk may be minimal on a six-string guitar, since vertical, homophonic "harp"-style improvisation involves several tones in one collective motion. With few alternate chords possible in the blues harmonic context (especially those in the piano-style blues), the accentuating homophonic chords would seem to become composed elements set in musical place.

David "Honeyboy" Edwards remembered that "[Johnson] didn't change his numbers much. Just like he'd play his first number he recorded, he'd play it the same way all the time. Every number that he played, it was just like he played it all the time. He never would do no changing too much."[103] It

---

[102] Shines 1975, 28
[103] Welding 1968, 9

would seem that Johnson has become a composer of guitar accompaniments so detailed as to preclude any free improvisation. On the other hand, he may have had yet to think of alternate homophonic chords to mix with the existing harmonic features.

Please Don't Block the Road

The lyrics for "Terraplane Blues" use the Hudson Terraplane automobile as a metaphor for a woman. In themselves, cars and the highways on which they were driven were replacing trains and railroads in imaginations everywhere. Completed, or nearly so, by 1935 were: Highway 49 (linking Helena through Clarksdale to Yazoo City, Jackson, Hattiesburg, and Gulfport), Highway 61 (wending along the western side of the Mississippi Delta, then continuing north through Memphis to St. Louis), Highway 80 (going east-west from Meridian through Jackson and Vicksburg), and Highway 82 (linking Greenville, Indianola, Greenwood, and Columbus).

Cars newer than used Model T or Model A Fords may have been difficult for many blacks to obtain, but they were worth buying for the ease and freedom from the rigid railroad schedules. Many people probably dreamed of having a powerful, stylish car to bring them to their destinations in the least time. As a result, state troopers or ("highway men") replaced riverboat pilots and railroad conductors in the bluesman's entreaties to not delay or slow down the journey. "Mr. Highway Man, please don't block the road" begged Johnson in "Terraplane Blues." Also using the Wheatstraw "Police Station Blues" theme for a highway blues was Big Joe Williams of Crawford, Mississippi, for "49 Highway Blues" in his 1935 debut session. Another car blues was Roosevelt Sykes's Mississippi-style "Highway 61 Blues." To a different theme and lyrics, Jack Kelly of Memphis recorded two renditions of his "Highway 61 Blues" in 1933.

Swapping and Stealing

Regarding "Terraplane Blues" and the other songs Johnson and his contemporaries knew in common, it is tempting to ascribe "tradition." As cordial as they were to one another, they also "stole" many musical themes and ideas from each other. As stated before, tradition was more a matter of "handing over" than "handing down." A look at the musicians around Helena in the mid-1930s suggests many covert borrowings among them. Johnny Shines remembered several unrecorded piano players there, including Robert Parnell, Piano Slim, and Roosevelt Caramac,[104] whose ideas were possibly lifted for use in guitar blues. Johnson was not the only guitar player in Mississippi listening to pianists live and on records. Elmore James appeared to have derived his style almost solely from Walter Roland's "Collector Man Blues" (1934), including his trademark high repeated tonic-note lick between lyric phrases.

Meanwhile, other notable bluesmen were also active around the mid-South. Howlin' Wolf at this time was switching from the guitar to the harmonica, adopting the tone of Aleck Miller, who would later call himself Sonny Boy Williamson (II) after John Lee Williamson. Miller was becoming a great harmonica technician, playing not only in second position "cross harp" (in the key of A on a D instrument), but also in third position (E Dorian mode) and fourth position (B Aeolian mode). Calvin Frazier, who knew Johnson and played with him for some years before his cousin Johnny Shines did, was an able guitarist who later produced recordings that sounded remarkably like Johnson. Around 1935 or early 1936 after a shooting scrape, he fled from Arkansas, first to Memphis where friends advised him to head north.[105]

Despite these associations, or maybe because of them, Johnson was very protective of his guitar techniques—especially of his Aadd9 tuning. If anyone else learned it, he may have feared that he

Photo by Edward Komara

Dwelling, Quito, MS

---

[104] Shines 1975, 25
[105] Rusch and Joyce 1978, 6; Earl 1973, 21

would have been in danger of becoming just another guitar player. Researchers have learned that Johnson, when in performance, would watch for anyone looking too intently at his hands; if he did spot someone, he would cut short the song or stop the set.[106] Apparently, he did not trust even Johnny Shines, who remembered many instances of him disappearing from his side and jumping to another town.[107] Any means of being heard and not seen must have seemed ideal to him.

Juke Boxes in the Delta

Records seemed to be the answer to Johnson's situation. Not only were records for home listening being purchased in increasing numbers again, they were appearing in public jukeboxes as well. The first jukeboxes were introduced in the early 1930s, and certainly before 1936 Johnson had to have seen one in St. Louis, where he became a friend with Henry Townsend.[108] The jukebox was wonderful because it was electrically amplified, capable of playing its records in a volume louder than most crowd noises. In addition, it only cost five cents to play one side. The chances for high sales, recognition, and musical dissemination for bluesmen through records multiplied with every jukebox installed.

The Audition for H.C. Speir

In October 1936, Johnson felt ready to fulfill his early ambition of getting paid to make commercial records. He went to Jackson and Speir's Music, where he knew he could find the talent scout that helped other musicians to land recording sessions.

H.C. Speir survived the worse years of the Great Depression with some changes in finances and industry associations. The money he had invested in the oil scheme in 1930 was lost when the well proved to be of natural gas, which was of little worth at the time.[109] Some of his contacts in the recording industry were lost when Paramount was closed and others shifted with the changes of ownership of Okeh.

Since 1932, Speir had worked with the American Recording Company. In 1934, he helped W. R. Calaway find Charlie Patton for the New York session.[110] During the following years, Speir conducted two commercial field recording sessions for A.R.C. in Jackson (1935) and Hattiesburg (1936). Whether Johnson knew of these recording sessions is uncertain, but it may have been just as well that he was absent from them. Of the 153 blues and sacred performances recorded at Hattiesburg, Calaway and A.R.C released only sixteen. Among the unreleased sides were the solo performances of the renowned pianist Cooney Vaughan, although he can be heard through his participation with the Graves brothers on the released Mississippi Jook Band sides. But Vaughan never had a chance to record after that and he was reported killed  sometime in the 1950s by a train, while passed out drunk on the tracks in Hattiesburg.[111] His death made the non-release and presumed junking of his solo sides all the more regrettable.

When Johnson presented himself at Speir's Music, the talent-broker listened. One biographer, Stephen LaVere,[112] believes the two went upstairs and made a demonstration disc, although whether it was to be an audition disc for A.R.C. or a vanity disc for Johnson is unclear. Years later, Speir remembered[113] only Johnson's falsetto—perhaps the high "ooh" in "Kind Hearted Woman" (see Fig. 32), or the "oh babe, my life feels all the same" passage in the third chorus—yet doubtless at the time he felt the young bluesman had much to offer. Instead of referring him to Calaway, who still owed money from the Hattiesburg sessions, Speir contacted Ernie Oertle, an A.R.C. sales representative for the mid-South region.[114] Somehow, Oertle heard Johnson, either on a demo disc or live in Jackson, and when he did, he offered the bluesman the opportunity to record for A.R.C. in San Antonio in November 1936.

---

[106] LaVere 1990, 13-14
[107] Shines 1970, 31, 33; 1975, 29
[108] Welding 1968
[109] Wardlow 1994, 32 n.11
[110] Calt and Wardlow 1988, 240
[111] Wardlow 1982, 8
[112] to Obrecht 1990b, 66
[113] Wardlow 1994, 15
[114] Wardlow 1994, 15; LaVere, 15

Fig. 32 – Robert Johnson, "Kind Hearted Woman Blues"

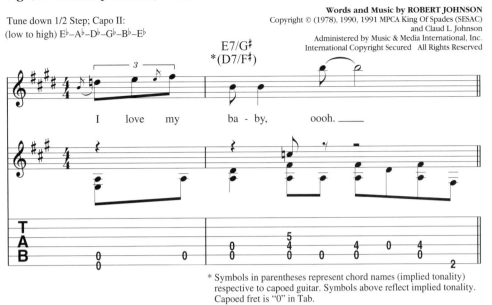

* Symbols in parentheses represent chord names (implied tonality)
respective to capoed guitar. Symbols above reflect implied tonality.
Capoed fret is "0" in Tab.

The First Session in San Antonio

Oertle drove Johnson to San Antonio, where they met producer Don Law, who would supervise the various artists in blues, country, and Mexican music that month. On November 23, Johnson made his first batch of commercial records, beginning with "Kind Hearted Woman Blues" and ending after eight more songs.

Don Law remembered the recording equipment was set up in the Gunter Hotel, although San Antonio researcher Lawrence Brown has since stated[115] that it was at the KONO radio station in the Blue Bonnet Hotel nearby. It was commercial studio quality, from the acetate-coated aluminum discs to the time limit indicator lights ("[Johnson would] tell me about things I'd never seen like 'start lights' and 'stop lights' used in recording," said Shines[116]).

On the records made during the November 23 session, Johnson sounds a bit nervous, which is to be expected. The first take of his first song, "Kind Hearted Woman Blues," is performed more than acceptably. In the fourth chorus, he plays a simple guitar solo. For someone so protective of his guitar technique, it is at first unthinkable for him to expose it nakedly through the open string tones, though it is in standard tuning. But the solo has a structural function to the overall performance. The take consists of five choruses that have a palindromic succession of themes (ABCBA). The relationship between the first and fifth choruses is clear, as they use the primary "Kind Hearted" theme. The guitar solo develops a lick played earlier at the end of the first lyric of the second chorus, and so in that way they are musically related. However, the tempo of take 2 is slightly faster, and he replaces the guitar solo with a vocal reprise of the main theme, thus altering the thematic succession to ABCAA. It isn't clear whether or not Johnson dropped the solo out of nervousness, or from a suggestion by Don Law.

He continued performing piano-style blues on "I Believe I'll Dust My Broom" (Aadd9), "Sweet Home Chicago" (standard), "Rambling on My Mind" (open E), and another treatment of the Davis "M. & O. Blues" theme, "When You Got a Good Friend," also in standard tuning (was Johnson really singing "Girl Friend"?). Interestingly, in the fourth chorus of take 1 of "Good Friend," Johnson lapses into the vocal melody of "Sweet Home Chicago," an easy thing to do since both songs share the same guitar accompaniment.

He then switched to open A tuning for his bottleneck piece "Come On in My Kitchen." Oddly, the two takes of "Kitchen" are in different tempi—the first in a relaxed string band pace of 70 beats per minute, the second in an uptempo, dance style of 108 beats per minute. He stayed in open A for "Terraplane Blues," this time in his plucked harmonica-style.

The two takes of the last song that afternoon, "Phonograph Blues," are a strange pair. The first take is in standard tuning and is in the manner of "Kind Hearted Woman Blues" in the key of B. The second

---

[115] to Jas Obrecht, 1990b, 66
[116] Earl 1973, 20

is in Aadd9 tuning in the key of E♭ at a slightly faster tempo, with the introduction of "When You Got a Good Friend" and in the style of "I Believe I'll Dust My Broom." What happened between takes, and why does Johnson sound somewhat rushed on the second one? A Law anecdote[117] may provide an answer: "[Law] asked him to play guitar for a group of Mexican musicians gathered in a hotel room where the recording equipment had been set up—Johnson turned his face to the wall, his back to the Mexican musicians." It has been pointed out by LaVere that Hermanas Barraza and his Mexican ensemble recorded after Johnson that day. It is a good bet that Johnson was preparing for one more take by adjusting his guitar to Aadd9 tuning when the Barraza band arrived. Rather than let them see his fretting technique, he turned himself around. He probably wasn't shy or embarrassed as Law believed in retelling this incident, but more likely he fell into his protective habit. If this indeed occurred, it had to have been between the two takes of "Phonograph Blues," and the second take captures Johnson's flustered unease at the situation.

But why would Johnson retune his guitar between takes of "Phonograph Blues" in the first place? Was he having technical and tuning problems with his instrument?

When the session's takes are replayed in matrix number (and presumably chronological) order, it may be noticed that Johnson's voice is fresh throughout, but oddly from time to time his guitar tone flattens, requiring retuning every other take. Had Johnson been so naive as to put on a new set of guitar strings the night before, recording before they were fully stretched? The following story told by Don Law to Frank Driggs in 1961, usually viewed with a bit of skepticism by some commentators, may help to explain the guitar pitch problems:

"Don Law considered himself responsible for Johnson, found him a room in a boarding house and told him to get some sleep so he would be ready to begin recording at ten the following morning. Law then joined his wife and some friends for dinner at the Gunter Hotel (sic). He had scarcely begun dinner when he was summoned to the phone. A policeman was calling from the city jail. Johnson had been picked up on a vagrancy charge. Law rushed down to the jail, found Johnson beat up, his guitar smashed; the cops had not only picked him up but had worked him over. With some difficulty, Law managed to get Johnson freed in his custody."

Johnson's first session was on a Monday. On the previous evening (Sunday), all music stores in San Antonio would have been closed. If his guitar had indeed been smashed, Johnson, with Law, would have had to buy a new instrument with fresh strings early the following morning, and then contend with the strings stretching out of tune during the session that day.

"Kind Hearted Woman" is in standard tuning in the key of A, but by the end of the second take the strings have slackened to A♭. For "I Believe I'll Dust My Broom" he adjusted the strings to Aadd9 tuning. Afterwards, he retuned to standard for "Sweet Home Chicago," then to open E for "Ramblin' on My Mind" over whose two takes the key goes from E to E♭. He returns to standard yet again for "Good Friend," and as before the strings slacken half a step during the two takes. He then switched to open A for "Come On in My Kitchen" and "Terraplane." With "Phonograph," he apparently decided to try one more piece in standard tuning, then after the first take he adjusts the inner strings to Aadd9.

During the course of the session, it would have made more sense to record all the standard-tuned pieces at once, but it may not have been possible to do that with the string problems on the guitar. Another possibility is that he may have insisted (or had been encouraged) on doing his most rehearsed and best tunes first, regardless of the retuning involved. With the frequent retunings and the nerve-wracking experience of a first session, Johnson must have felt exhausted and perhaps a little frustrated at the end of the day. The individual takes, however, sound excellent, and at the time of recording must have been considered of contemporary commercial value, as each were current blues piano themes arranged for and adeptly played on guitar and sung to fresh lyrics.

The Second and Third Sessions in San Antonio

Johnson was given two days off, which he may have spent preparing and rehearsing additional songs. In contrast to the current piano blues melodies recorded on the first day, most of what he performed on November 26 and 27 were Mississippi guitar blues, including ones derived from Son House and Charlie Patton. On November 26, in between sessions by the Chuck Wagon Gang and Andres

---

[117] Driggs 1961

Berlanga, Johnson quickly did "32-20 Blues," his adaptation of the Skip James piano record. During the following day, he recorded seven songs, leading off with the hokum number "They're Red Hot." He then proceeded to play "Dead Shrimp Blues," which is the "Kind Hearted Woman Blues" melody set to new lyrics. Perhaps at this time he believed "Kind Hearted Woman Blues" would be a hit and wanted to have a disguised second version of the theme ready in the wake of eventual success.

"Cross Road Blues (Crossroads)"

Then he turned to "Cross Road Blues," tuning his guitar to open A. As discussed earlier, the basic theme is that of Leroy Carr's "Straight Alky Blues" and Roosevelt Sykes's derivative "Black River Blues," but Johnson alters much of the melody after the first chorus almost beyond cursory recognition. Carr and Sykes sang the theme in the relaxed urban manner of starting phrases on the first measure downbeat or on the upbeat in the "pickup" measure preceding the chorus. Johnson resets it in the rural field holler phrasing of an ax-fall downbeat rest and then the phrase, as in the words "Asked the Lord above 'have mercy'" (both takes, first chorus) and "I tried to flag a ride" (second take, second chorus):

Fig. 33A – Robert Johnson, "Cross Road Blues (Crossroads)"

Open A Tuning; Down 1/2 Step; Capo II:
(low to high) E♭–A♭–E♭–A♭–C–E♭

Words and Music by ROBERT JOHNSON
Copyright © (1978), 1990, 1991 MPCA King Of Spades (SESAC)
and Claud L. Johnson
Administered by Music & Media International, Inc.
International Copyright Secured   All Rights Reserved

* Symbols in parentheses represent chord names (implied tonality) respective to capoed guitar.
Symbols above reflect implied tonality. Capoed fret is "0" in Tab.

Fig. 33B – Robert Johnson, "Cross Road Blues (Crossroads)"

Open A Tuning; Down 1/2 Step; Capo II:
(low to high) E♭–A♭–E♭–A♭–C–E♭

Words and Music by ROBERT JOHNSON
Copyright © (1978), 1990, 1991 MPCA King Of Spades (SESAC)
and Claud L. Johnson
Administered by Music & Media International, Inc.
International Copyright Secured   All Rights Reserved

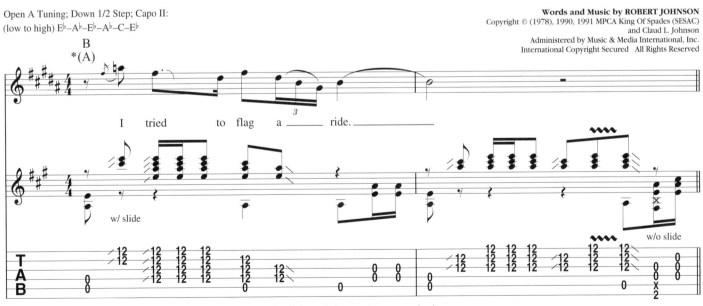

* Symbols in parentheses represent chord names (implied tonality) respective to capoed guitar.
Symbols above reflect implied tonality. Capoed fret is "0" in Tab.

Accompanying himself in his "harp" style of guitar, Johnson, in the second version, takes special pains to use the I–I7–I type of fill at the end of each chorus's first phrase (Fig. 34A), the I–vi–I type at the end of the second phrase (Fig. 34B), and the open I chord at the end of the third and final phrase (Fig. 34C).

Fig. 34 – Robert Johnson, "Cross Road Blues (Crossroads)"
take 2, harmonica-style fill chords

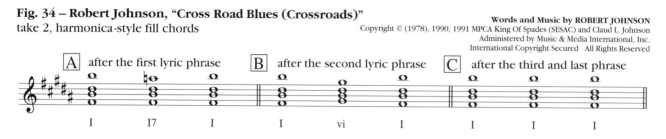

During the vocal passages, Johnson plays a guitar equivalent of the "slapping hands—patting his hands, blowing and singing" that Shines recalled of his Highway 61 playing. Instead of a thumbed common-time bass, he uses a brief bass figure on the 5th string (Fig. 35A) or an alternation between percussive bass notes (35B) to replicate the sound of his hands slapping and patting his arms and thighs.

Fig. 35A – Robert Johnson, "Cross Road Blues (Crossroads)"
take 2, ch. 2, fifth string bass figure, at the word "boy"

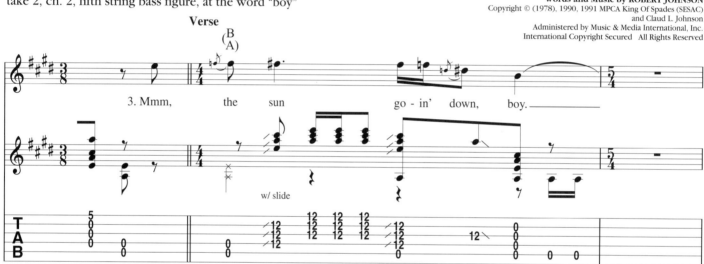

Fig. 35B – Robert Johnson, "Cross Road Blues (Crossroads)"
take 2, ch. 2, alternating beats, at the words "everybody pass me by"

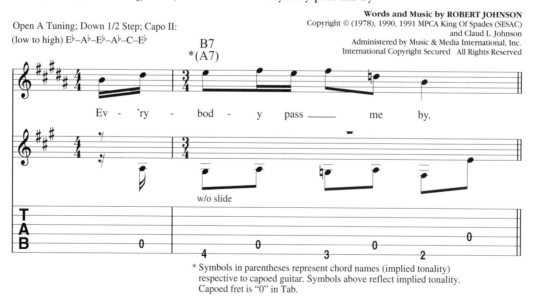

* Symbols in parentheses represent chord names (implied tonality) respective to capoed guitar. Symbols above reflect implied tonality. Capoed fret is "0" in Tab.

There are two takes of "Cross Road Blues": the first was at a rushed tempo of 116 beats per minute, and the second was at a restrained pace of 96 beats per minute that allows every note and chord to be heard. The first take was issued in May 1937, yet the second take has been more the focus of scrutiny since its 1961 issue on the famous *King of the Delta Blues Singers* LP and through its subsequent notated transcriptions. When the first take was widely reissued in 1990, its faster tempo and extra chorus afforded an intriguing comparative study, especially on chorus openings (see Fig. 36). The first chorus openings are alike, but the openings for other choruses differ between takes; it is rare to hear Johnson using such a variety of chorus openings. Although both takes are in the same key, the pitch range in take 1 is higher than in take 2, and the slower second take allows each syllable to be enunciated with more pitches, as can be seen in the opening for chorus 4.

Fig. 36A – Robert Johnson, "Cross Road Blues (Crossroads)"
verse openings for take 1, vocal only

Fig. 36B – Robert Johnson, "Cross Road Blues (Crossroads)"
verse openings for take 2, vocal only

Johnson had to be careful about keeping elements of "Terraplane Blues" out of "Cross Road Blues." Both blues are played "harp" style in open A tuning, and in both songs Johnson uses the single bottle-neck-fretted bass tone at the dominant V chord (see Chapt. 2, Fig. 7A). In take 1 of "Cross Road Blues," he often uses a lick (Fig. 37A) that is very close to the "Terraplane Blues" motif (Fig. 37B). In take 2, however, he refrains from its use (except in the third chorus), perhaps to lessen its confusion with "Terraplane" and to lend "Cross Road Blues" a stylistic consistency of its own.

Fig. 37A – Robert Johnson, "Cross Road Blues (Crossroads)"
take 1, guitar fill lick

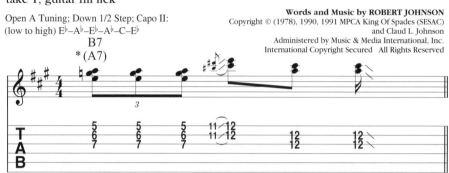

* Symbols in parentheses represent chord names (implied tonality) respective to capoed guitar.
Symbols above reflect implied tonality. Capoed fret is "0" in Tab.

Fig. 37B – Robert Johnson, "Terraplane Blues,"
guitar fill lick, similar to 37a

* Symbols in parentheses represent chord names (implied tonality) respective to capoed guitar.
Symbols above reflect implied tonality. Capoed fret is "0" in Tab.

The two performances of "Cross Road Blues" show Johnson's means of vertical homophonic development at a more refined level than what had been observed for "The Last Fair Deal Gone Down" and "Kind Hearted Woman Blues." His "blues harp" style of guitar allows him to embed various chords and motifs within the melodic and harmonic structures, and affords more musical devices in each chorus than what was possible in his piano-style accompaniments. In "Cross Road Blues," he seemed to have included all that he could from the types of blues associated with the piano, guitar, and harmonica. To go beyond would be to include in the "Cross Road" fills bits from other types of music outside the blues. But for now, in these particular takes, Johnson is heard at the top of his improvisational skills—switching chords, motifs, and chorus openings—yet retaining certain melodic features in all choruses to ensure musical unity.

By singing the urban blues theme of "Cross Road Blues" in a rural manner, Johnson indicates the choice among his generation between staying "down home" and living with racial bias and economic poverty or moving to the cities to the north, if need be, for better possibilities. Yet Johnson is not sounding like Leroy Carr or Charlie Patton; through his densely packed alterations and additions, he presents his own expression as a product of his musical balance between rural and urban styles. Commentators have long dwelled on the supposed supernatural aspects of the lyrics, although those same words may also be interpreted as about hitchhiking. Johnson, as a mover within the ongoing demographic shift of blacks in the 1930s, may not have expected or wanted his lines to become reliable historical documents. As a master musician, though, he would offer his blues as a leading means of expression during those changing times. For all that it includes and indicates, "Cross Road Blues" is Johnson at his greatest.

The rest of the November 27 session continued with older, guitar-based repertory; this included "Walking Blues," "The Last Fair Deal Gone Down," "Preaching Blues," and "If I Had Possession Over

Judgment Day." "Walking Blues" and "Preaching Blues" were treatments of the Son House blues of six years earlier, but here Johnson resets them with the bass accompaniment techniques that he developed in the meantime. Also, "Preaching" and "Possession" are singular examples of bottleneck slide—especially "Preaching" with its quotes (see Chapter 3, Fig. 10) and interpolations. All in all, the whole session went very well (with none of the pitch problems of the first session) and Johnson was comfortable enough with the recording process to give some superlative performances within the three minute time limit.

A Hit Record and a Hiatus

The first record released, "Terraplane Blues" b/w "Kind Hearted Woman Blues," became a hit on its appearance in March 1937. Son House heard it in Robinsonville: "We heard a couple of his pieces come out on records. Believe the first one I heard was 'Terraplane Blues.' Jesus, it was good! We all admired it. Said, 'That boy is really going places.'"[118]

The record caught the attention of a white reviewer as well. Writing for the left-wing newspaper *The New Masses* (2 March 1937, 29) under the pseudonym "Henry Johnson," young New York music scout and promoter John Hammond hailed Johnson as "the greatest Negro blues singer who has cropped up in recent years." Impishly he added, "Johnson makes Leadbelly sound like an accomplished poseur."

On the strength of that success, ARC issued more Johnson releases in the ensuing months. In April, there were two discs. "I Believe I'll Dust My Broom" b/w "Dead Shrimp Blues" on one, and "32–20 Blues" b/w "The Last Fair Deal Gone Down" on the other. In May came "Cross Road Blues" b/w "Ramblin' on My Mind." These issues did not have the phenomenal success of "Terraplane," but they must have maintained ARC's faith in Johnson as a record personality.

That same spring, Johnson and Johnny Shines went north with Calvin Frazier, who was persuaded to move to Canada to evade any possible retaliation for the 1935 shooting incident in Arkansas. Upon reaching northern Michigan, they met Elder Moten, a well-known preacher in Detroit and Windsor, Ontario, who invited Johnson and Shines to perform on his radio hour. Afterwards, Frazier decided to stay in Detroit. The other two travelers proceeded to Chicago and St. Louis, although later Shines recalled losing Johnson in Detroit and catching up with him in New York.[119] In July 1937 (instead of 1935 or 1936 as he recalled to Pete Welding),[120] Johnson told Shines of a recording session in Dallas. Shines wanted to come along, but upon seeing that Johnson already had a train ticket, he decided to meet him there later.

New Songs for Dallas

Johnson brought two new blues to the Dallas sessions. One was "Stop Breakin' Down," closely patterned after Memphis Minnie's 1936 "Caught Me Wrong Again." Her record was the latest in the melodic trend of AB (four measures + eight measures) chorus blues that had come to widespread use with Tampa Red's "Tight Like That" in 1929. Memphis Minnie and her then-partner Kansas Joe McCoy adopted the chorus scheme in many records such as "Going Back to Texas" (1930) and "You Ain't Got to Move" (1934). In 1935, singer Buddy Moss recorded "Stop Hanging Around;" this used the same four+ eight chorus scheme and a similar melody to that used by Minnie and McCoy. Johnson probably wished to use the most up-to-date version of this chorus, which may be why he borrowed Minnie's vocal mannerisms and common-time instrumental accompaniment from "Caught Me Wrong Again" in particular.

Another blues he prepared was "Love in Vain." Its melodic basis was "When the Sun Goes Down," first recorded by Leroy Carr in February 1935 during what was to be his last session before dying from the effects of alcoholism. Before the year was over, Amos Easton, Josh White, and Memphis Minnie each made cover versions. Johnson replaced the original lyrics with a wistful narrative of seeing a love departing on a train. One lyric element, the "two lights on behind," has been pointed out by some commentators as having appeared on Blind Lemon

---

[118] House to Lester 1965, 42
[119] Earl 1973, 21
[120] Welding 1970

Jefferson's 1927 "Dry Southern Blues," but the same phrase turns up on a Decca release from early 1937, Black Ivory King's "Flying Crow Blues."[121]

The distinguishing melodic aspect of "When the Sun Goes Down" is the descending title statement in measure 11 of each chorus, attached to the main phrase beginning in measure 9. Johnson retains this feature in his "Love in Vain" (Fig. 38A), where it is similar in form and function to the added phrases in each line of "Hell Hound on My Trail" (Fig. 38B). This shared characteristic of new and old blues may indicate an advanced stylistic mastery over his varied repertory.

Fig. 38A – Robert Johnson's attached phrases from "Love in Vain Blues"

Fig. 38B – Robert Johnson, "Hell Hound on My Trail," attached phrases

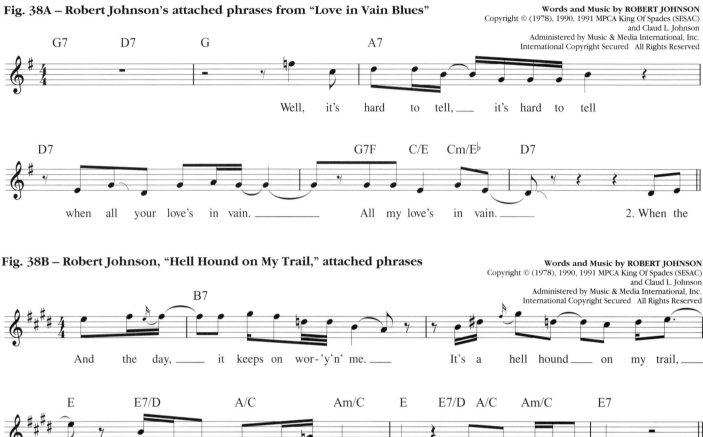

The Dallas sessions were held in the ARC warehouse with much the same equipment and procedures used in San Antonio the previous year. Johnson and the technicians—including producer Don Law—must have greeted each other with familiarity and confidence. That July, ARC had issued "Come On in My Kitchen" b/w "They're Red Hot," and it was preparing a fifth coupling, "Sweet Home Chicago" b/w "Walking Blues," for release the following month. Everyone must have felt ready to try recording a few more potential hits.

The First Dallas Session

The first session, on July 19, seems concerned with duplicating the "Terraplane"/"Kind Hearted" pairing that had sold so well. Interestingly, Johnson and the recording team seemed uninterested in new versions of "Dust My Broom," "Sweet Home Chicago," or "Ramblin' on My Mind," perhaps because none had sold on the level of "Terraplane." Ironically, those three would be among the more covered Johnson songs by rock musicians in the 1960s, no doubt due to their boogie patterns. "Stones In My Passway" was "Terraplane" with new lyrics. Although "I'm a Steady Rollin' Man" was sung in the manner of Peetie Wheatstraw's "Johnnie Blues" (1935), it was accompanied in the "Kind Hearted Woman Blues" standard-tuned guitar setting. Before leaving for the day, he did "From Four Until Late," the old "Betty and Dupree" tune that could date from his Hazlehurst days.

---

[121] Groom 1976 (July/August), 16

The Second Dallas Session

The following day was an extended session in which Johnson performed his oldest and his latest blues. He began with "Hell Hound on My Trail" and "Little Queen of Spades," then revived his "Robert Lonnie" days with "Malted Milk" and "Drunken Hearted Man" in the manner of Lonnie Johnson. "Me and the Devil Blues" came next, then the new piece "Stop Breakin' Down." Johnson's studio professionalism throughout these sides is consistent; sometimes the only difference between two takes of a given piece like "Little Queen of Spades" or "Drunken Hearted Man" is a slightly muffed line or a garbled word.

The session continued with "Traveling Riverside Blues" and its "Roll and Tumble" guitar adornments. "Honeymoon Blues," based melodically on the secondary theme of "Kind Hearted Women Blues," uses the piano-style chime to suggest wedding bells at the start of the first chorus. The next song, "Love in Vain," seems stark by comparison; it may have been so new that no special licks had yet been added. In addition, despite popular belief all these years that it is in standard tuning (as the Rolling Stones performed it), it is Johnson's only song in open G (Spanish) tuning. Why he decided to play in this common Delta tuning at this point in his life is still a mystery, however it may help to explain the considerable string muting present. Because of its instrumental simplicity, the heartbreaking narrative is all the more clearly memorable. To round out the session, Johnson did another treatment of the "Terraplane" melody and accompaniment for good measure, this time to the "Milkcow" lyric concept then widely used. There is nothing in "Milkcow's Calf Blues" to indicate it was to be Johnson's last recording song; in fact, its perfunctory performances seem to suggest that he, Law, and the ARC technicians expected to work together again sometime soon.

If the keys and guitar tunings suggested for the 1937 Dallas sessions are correct, it appears Johnson did not use (or did not have to use) a capo during the entire session. One possibility is he lost his capo before arriving in Dallas. Another is he was playing a twelve-fret guitar and adjusted his repertoire (and tunings) accordingly. In addition, he used his slide sparingly on "Stop Breakin' Down," "Traveling Riverside Blues," and "Milkcow's Calf Blues."

The Last Sessions: Were they Better than We Now Think?

Recent critics have had mixed views on Johnson's 1937 sides: "Naturally, there are a few duds"[122] and "These last dates included both his most inspired and his most derivative recordings."[123] Wishing for another classic performance on the level of "Cross Road Blues," some[124] have taken "Hell Hound on My Trail" as a masterpiece. "Hell Hound" is a memorable performance, but its flaws, noted earlier in the discussion of Skip James's "Yola My Blues Away," cannot be dismissed; and it offers fewer musical contrasts and possibilities than "Cross Road Blues." What may be one source of disappointment is that Johnson recorded more of the older blues in 1937, styles which have since been rendered obsolete by later developments in blues and rock. A record like "Malted Milk" or "Little Queen of Spades" may have been perceived at the time of release as having been sung with a sense of feeling and irony; that sense would be lost on listeners today. For this, do not blame Johnson, but rather the changes in musical trends and tastes over the last seventy years.

A Kansas City Detour

One month before the Dallas sessions, the "Sight and Sound" column of *The New Masses* (8 June 1937) briefly mentioned Johnson as the "Hot Springs' star" from Robinsonville. Again, the reviewer was John Hammond, this time writing under his own name. That little spark of national recognition may have been but a small surviving result of Johnson's unceasing travels and ARC's monthly releases

---

[122] LaVere 1990, 21
[123] Guralnick 1982, 35
[124] especially Guralnick 1982, 36, and Obrecht 1990b, 70

of his records. Much of ARC's distribution was limited to the South, so when Hammond learned about Johnson, he had to get his copies of the records from a southern distributor.[125]

Incidentally, Hammond in 1937 was also taking a strong interest in the Count Basie Band of Kansas City, Missouri, which had tenor saxophonist Lester Young and drummer Jo Jones.[126] On free nights, Jones would play in free-for-all jam sessions where the ridicule was harsher than any criticism, and he would provide the worst derision by "gonging" a soloist the same way it was done on the popular Major Bowes Amateur Hour radio show. One of Jones's victims, a seventeen year old high school dropout named Charlie Parker, was so embarrassed that he was not seen around Kansas City for the rest of the summer of 1937. When he was seen again that fall, Parker had dramatically improved enough to secure some of his first paying band jobs. Later, during the 1940s, he would become a bebop pioneer changing the sound of jazz. In 1950, Parker recounted somewhat sheepishly his Reno Club humiliation to Marshall Stearns and John Maher.[127] After his death in 1955, the story of his shame, absence, and improvement in 1937 was confirmed by Gene Ramey,[128] who revealed that Parker had spent that summer playing under a strict bandleader at an Ozark resort, much like Johnson under Zinnerman at Hazlehurst. However, Parker never claimed, nor has anyone has ever dared to suggest, that he sold his soul to the devil to play the way he did.

Transitions

For the rest of the summer, Johnson returned to his performance rounds, from Helena through Friar's Point, where old friends Hard Rock and Elizabeth Glynn tried to have him play at their juke.[129] He also ventured to Greenwood and nearby Itta Bena, where he made acquaintance with David "Honey Boy" Edwards[130] who, in later years, would imitate his songs.

During the harvest season, the first records from Johnson's Dallas sessions began to appear: "Hell Hound on My Trail" b/w "From Four Until Late" in September, and "Malted Milk" b/w "Milkcow's Calf Blues" the next month. Neither disc sold well, nor did "Stones in My Passway" b/w "I'm a Steady Rollin' Man" at Christmas time. ARC kept up its promotion of Johnson in 1938, releasing "Stop Breakin' Down" b/w "Honeymoon Blues" and "Me and the Devil Blues" b/w "Little Queen of Spades" during the spring. Wherever he went, he could refer to a new record release to those who saw him regularly.

Johnson did not record again. Most writers have attributed this to the relatively poor sales of his releases after "Terraplane Blues." However, the record industry was still slow in rebuilding, with unit sales at 33 million discs sold in 1938—one third the level before the Depression.[131] Johnson's records sold as well as expected for their time and limited distribution, and their later rarity may be due to unsold stock later scrapped for shellac towards the World War II effort. A more likely reason for Johnson not recording again may have been the changes at ARC. It did not hold a field session in the southwest until December 1938, at which time the ARC/Brunswick conglomeration was purchased by the Columbia Broadcasting System (CBS).[132] Presumably, the negotiations and changes that come with such a sale may have shuffled accounting, distribution, and personnel for some while. In any event, the "Me and the Devil" release was the last Johnson was to see.

Death in the Delta

On September 26, 1937, the great blues singer Bessie Smith died in a horrible auto accident on Highway 61 a little north of Clarksdale. According to Dr. Hugh Smith, who came upon the scene while driving on an early morning fishing trip, her driver sideswiped a truck resting on the right side of the narrow highway. In the collision, Smith's right arm was nearly severed, and her right side sustained "severe crushing injuries." She was pronounced dead at the G.T. Thomas Hospital for blacks in Clarksdale.[133]

However, rumors of Smith being denied treatment at a white hospital soon found their way into print. Working with what he heard from Chick Webb bandmembers, John Hammond wrote an article

[125] Driggs 1961
[126] Hammond 1977, 165-171
[127] a full transcription of this interview is in Woideck 1998, 109
[128] Reisner 1962, 185-186
[129] Calt and Wardlow 1989, 47
[130] Welding 1968, 8
[131] Dixon, Godrich, and Rye 1997, xxiii
[132] Dixon, Godrich, and Rye, xxxiii
[133] Albertson 1972, 219-223

in an October 1937 issue of *Downbeat,* "Did Bessie Smith Bleed to Death While Waiting for Medical Aid?"[134] Only in 1972 could Smith biographer Chris Albertson present a cogent account of her death.

Undoubtedly, Johnson heard about Smith's death, rumors and all. In addition to reminding him of the perils of a bluesman's life, the incident may have shown him how the circumstances of one's death can overshadow the musical achievements of that lifetime. Even Charlie Patton, one of the few bluesmen to have died from natural causes, was rumored to have been knifed to death or even struck by lightning.[135] In those days, there was little radio or newspaper reportage in Mississippi about blacks for blacks, and in the remote areas in the Delta there was none. News was unreliably passed through word of mouth. Relying as he did on oral publicity wherever he played, Johnson may have sensed that this method would spread the true and false stories of his eventual death, with the likely result of his name becoming better known for non-musical reasons.

Johnson died on August 16, 1938 on a plantation near Greenwood after events that are still mysterious. The Mississippi Bureau of Vital Statistics recorded on the death certificate the plantation owner's opinion that he died from syphilis. However, rumors have abounded of death by outright poisoning (or pneumonia after an attempted poisoning) committed by a jealous girlfriend or a jealous husband,[136] with the events supposedly set in motion by the devil reclaiming Johnson's soul.[137]

Marker for purported Johnson grave, Payne Chapel cemetary, Quito, MS. In addition to this and the Mt. Zion site near Morgan City, a third site north of Greenwood has been cited as possible.

Throughout his musical life, Johnson perceived and learned the major blues trends of his day and replicated them on his guitar. During his recording sessions he proved himself a versatile musician who possessed a varied repertoire that contained some musical continuity among some songs. Upon his death, his possession was loosened, and the individual melodies and instrumental devices returned to the trends from which they were taken. Some of his contemporaries like Big Joe Williams and Bukka White pursued and performed the tunes they had in common with Johnson. Those who were personally influenced by him would pick up his fallen musical torch and carry it through the times to come.

---

[134] Albertson 1972, 216
[135] Wardlow 1967, 12
[136] LaVere 1990, 18; Calt and Wardlow 1989, 49-50
[137] Guralnick 1982, 36

CHAPTER SEVEN

Musical Highways and Byways after Robert Johnson

The Aftermath of Johnson's Death

The bad news of Robert Johnson's death and the accompanying rumors spread slowly through the Delta during the fall of 1938. Johnny Shines first learned about it from Aleck "Sonny Boy Williamson" Miller, who claimed that Johnson died in his arms. Only when the death was confirmed by Honey Boy Edwards (who also claimed to have been there) did Shines realize Johnson was gone.[138]

Also affected was John Hammond, who learned of Johnson's death through Don Law. Hammond was engaging artists for his "From Spirituals to Swing" concert scheduled for December 23, 1938, and he had been keen to bring Johnson to Carnegie Hall on this occasion. As a substitute, he booked Big Bill Broonzy, an ARC/Vocalion artist who had recorded his own reworking of Tampa Red's "Gravy" theme and of the Mississippi Sheiks' "Sitting on Top of the World."[139] During the concerts, Hammond played Johnson's recordings of "Walking Blues" and the then unissued "Preaching Blues" from the stage on a phonograph.[140] It may have been from Hammond's act that ARC released its last Johnson 78, "Preaching Blues" b/w "Love in Vain" by or around March 1939.[141]

Like Hammond, listeners following the current blues styles through Johnson's records now had to turn to other musicians for the latest settings and variants. To be sure, Johnson was not alone in his musical progress, and many of his Mississippi and Arkansas blues contemporaries continued to use the melodies they shared with him.

The New Masses Presents
AN EVENING OF AMERICAN NEGRO MUSIC
"From Spirituals to Swing"
[DEDICATED TO BESSIE SMITH]
CONCEIVED AND PRODUCED BY
John Hammond
DIRECTED BY
Charles Friedman

American Negro music as it was invented, developed, sung, played and heard by the Negro himself—the true, untainted folk song, spirituals, work songs, songs of protest, chain gang songs, Holy Roller chants, shouts, blues, minstrel music, honky-tonk piano, early jazz, and finally, the contemporary swing of Count Basie, presented by the greatest living artists from the South, the Southwest, and Negro communities in the North. The first comprehensive concert of the true and exciting music of the Negro. With pianists Meade Lux Lewis, Albert Ammons, Pete Johnson, James P. Johnson; blues singers Ruby Smith, Robert Johnson; Mitchell's Christian Singers; finest Negro dancers.

Count Basie
AND HIS ORCHESTRA

Willie Bryant, Master of Ceremonies

FRIDAY EVENING, DECEMBER 23, 1938
Carnegie Hall
SEVENTH AVENUE AND 57th STREET, NEW YORK CITY

All seats reserved: $1.10, $1.75, $2.20, $2.65, $1.10, $1.65 cents; New Masses, 31 East 27th Street, N.Y.C. and Carnegie Hall

Calvin Frazier

Did Johnson engender a blues tradition? This seems hard to believe, in view of his secrecy in developing his guitar technique and his cautious performing habits. The musicians after him who tried performing his songs on one guitar usually had to leave their bass figures to play their treble licks, or enlisted additional musicians to maintain the bass accompaniment. In addition, since Johnson seems to have not recorded a melodic theme of his own devising, it appears his imitators have unwittingly carried the melodic traditions of Leroy Carr, Roosevelt Sykes, Peetie Wheatstraw, and Walter Davis.

Calvin Frazier, Johnny Shines, and Robert Jr. Lockwood are possibly the only musicians who figured out Johnson's piano-style technique. In October 1938, two months after Johnson's death, Frazier and another guitarist, Sampson Pittman, made some recordings in Detroit for Alan Lomax and the Library of Congress. Among the performances Frazier gave was "This Whole World's in a Tangle," accompanying himself with Johnson's piano-style guitar technique.

Frazier continued performing for the rest of his life, recording rarely and with little if any use of the Johnson technique. During his Savoy session in 1951, he played single-note electric guitar solos in front of a small jump-style band. Later recordings with Washboard Willie appear to indicate little of his

[138] Obrecht 1990a, 29
[139] Hammond 1977, 202
[140] Hammond 1938, 27
[141] LaVere 1990, 15, has the same release date

old acoustic style. A 1971 interview with George Paulus in *Blues Unlimited* caught a bit of Frazier's undiminished regard for Johnson: "Motherfucker (sic)—that Robert!" he exclaimed while listening to a Johnson reissue. He died in 1972.

Johnny Shines

Frazier's cousin Johnny Shines had missed his early opportunity to record in 1937, as he found Johnson in Red Water, Texas, after the Dallas sessions; he simply arrived too late.[142] He eventually secured his first chance to record in 1946 for a Columbia session that was long unissued. He then made his first released single in 1950 for Chess. But it was for J.O.B. Records in 1952 that he made his covers of Johnson's "Walking Blues" and "Terraplane Blues," respectively retitled "Ramblin'" and "Fish Tail." These two sides show off Shines's bottleneck nuances on the fretboard—the very feature of Johnson's playing to which Shines was initially attracted. On "Fish Tail" (as in the "Fish Tail" Cadillac then popular), Shines executes a fair approximation of Johnson's "harp" style; however, he tended to strum the strings rather than pluck them. Of those who knew Johnson, Shines was the best-spoken, pointing out the intervals that the legendary musician had used and sharing what he learned or figured out.[143] He retained his enviable bottleneck touch and his powerful tenor voice until his death in 1992.

Honeyboy Edwards

David "Honeyboy" Edwards is so much associated with Robert Johnson that his acknowledged ties with the Mississippi Sheiks and Big Joe Williams are often forgotten. Although he has since had a few commercial sessions, several of his 1941-1942 recordings for Alan Lomax and the Library of Congress remain among his best known. Edwards shared Johnson's admiration for Walter Davis, as evident in his Library of Congress recording "Water Coast Blues," a rendition of Davis's "West Coast Blues." He often replays Johnson blues in standard tuning with a bottleneck, sometimes abandoning the bass strings during a treble fill. Despite his limited technique, he has provided much information about the musical times of his youth.[144]

Robert Jr. Lockwood

Through the years, Robert Jr. Lockwood acknowledged his lessons with Johnson, although he commented on few specific points. To Mit Schuller (1975) he revealed, "Robert Johnson could play like Lonnie Johnson. Things by Lonnie Johnson that I learned, I learned from Robert, who could play like anyone he wanted." It is likely that Johnson taught what he learned from Ike Zinnerman a few years before and gave a firm musical foundation on which Lockwood would develop his jazz guitar style.

Lockwood learned enough of Johnson's fretting technique to record several blues in the piano-style manner for Victor Bluebird in 1941. His ability to maintain the bass accompaniment during the treble licks is evident on these takes, despite the bassist (or tub-bassist) obscuring the lower range of Lockwood's guitar. "Black Spider Blues" is based on "Kind Hearted Woman Blues" with Johnson's chime chords and other licks associated with this tune. "I'm Gonna Train My Baby" uses a different melody, but it retains the "Kind Hearted Woman" guitar accompaniment and the Amos Easton-style contrasting theme. The initial choruses of "Take a Little Walk with Me" are clearly based on "Sweet Home Chicago," although in the third and later choruses the first four measures are substituted with the opening bars of Bukka White's "Shake 'Em on Down." Johnson commentator Bob Groom reported learning from Lockwood that "Black Spider Blues" and "Take a Little Walk" were originally Robert Johnson blues.[145] If so, the possible date of composition for "Black Spider" is uncertain, but "Take a Little Walk," with its "Shake 'Em on Down" opening phrases, may date from 1938.

---

[142] Shines 1970, 31
[143] as in Earl 1973, 13
[144] see Welding 1968 and Edwards 1997
[145] Groom 1976 (July/August) 17

Another song that Lockwood said he learned from Johnson was "Mr. Downchild."[146] This blues has been most strongly associated with Sonny Boy Williamson II, who was known to have played in Helena with Johnson in the 1930s. Whether Johnson learned the song from Miller or vice versa is not clear, and on his recorded performances Miller slightly distorts the theme with his own vocal inflections. The melodic basis for "Mr. Downchild" appears to be "Sweet Home Chicago," as recently demonstrated by Robert Lockwood in the film "Can't You Hear the Wind Howl?" Sonny Boy and Lockwood may have played this song often on their legendary "King Biscuit Time" radio broadcasts on KFFA in Helena through 1943. In 1960, they recorded it for Chess (Sonny Boy did a famous version for Trumpet in 1951). Lockwood died in 2006.

Robert Johnson, Electric Blues Guitarist?

There is a recollection of Johnson performing with a pianist and a drummer in Belzoni,[147] and another of him playing the recently developed electric guitar in 1938.[148] Whether he was a pioneer in these kinds of accompaniment, or just trying out instruments that were already at hand in Helena and elsewhere, is an unsettled question. Considering that Johnson may have been the only guitarist of the 1930s to successfully play the bass and treble lines simultaneously, his fellow guitarists may have long had to work with other instrumentalists in order to perform in the piano style regularly.

Elmore James, Electric Blues Guitarist

Elmore James comes most readily to mind when thinking of Mississippi bluesmen who employed additional musical help, and his presence in Johnson's musical company muddies the blues attribution waters. A guitarist of modest harmonic ability, he was capable of producing ringing tones high up on the fretboard, whether on an acoustic guitar or later on an electric one. But he always needed a backup band, usually a second guitar or piano, bass, and drums to provide a foundation for his high-octave licks. He was as severely limited in his repertory as with his technique, and many of his records made between his 1951 debut session and his 1963 death follow the rhythmic pattern, harmonic progression, lyric scheme, and melodic fills of Walter Roland's "Collector Man Blues."

James's first recording, "Dust My Broom" for Trumpet in August 1951, contains much of musical dispute. A casual listen reveals the bass and drums maintaining a basic common time accompaniment, with James singing the theme and harpist Sonny Boy Williamson II playing the "Collector Man" riff. However, Robert Lockwood had recorded his first version of "Dust My Broom" the previous March for J.O.B. (who inexplicably did not release it at the time), then did a second version for Mercury in November 1951, a month or two after the release of James's Trumpet rendition. Both of Lockwood's performances have the same characteristics as James's, except that the harmonica player is replaced with pianist Sunnyland Slim. Lockwood[149] felt at the time of the Mercury session (and afterward) that Johnson wrote the song.

When Johnson's 1936 version is played, the swinging quarter note boogie bass and the triplet eighth note lick at the high octave can be heard. But, as noted earlier, the melody appeared in 1932 on a Sparks Brothers release on Victor, and the high triplet fill was used by Walter Roland on "Collector Man Blues":

---

[146] Groom 1976 (July/August) 17
[147] LaVere 1990, 20
[148] Obrecht 1990b, 71
[149] Hoffman 1995

Fig. 39 – Walter Roland, "Collector Man Blues"

It becomes a question of who combined the melody and fills: Johnson, James, or someone else they both listened to. If Lockwood was correct in naming Johnson as the composer, then it is odd that Johnson never used "Dust My Broom" as the basis for another record (not counting the rushed second take of "Phonograph Blues"). It wasn't that boogie tunes were not popular numbers in Johnson's song bag. They certainly had to have been, but Johnson's "Terraplane Blues" with its harp-style accompaniment was apparently such a successful novelty that he repeated its formula in 1937 towards producing another hit record. On the other hand, James used "Collector Man"/"Dust My Broom" as the basis for nearly everything else he was to record. There is a strong certainty that Elmore James simply took the song lock, stock, and barrel from Johnson when both were performing in Belzoni in 1937 and 1938. Yet there is the possibility both men took the song from Walter Roland or Roland imitators in the mid-1930s. The musical trends these versions of "Dust My Broom" had in common were widespread enough in recorded blues in the early- to mid-1930s that any possibility among as-yet unrecorded musicians in Mississippi and the Mid-South could have happened. This problem in the authorship of "Dust My Broom" goes to show how competitive the blues circles in Memphis, Helena, and the Mississippi Delta had become. No wonder Johnson was so secretive about his craft.

Son House Redux

When John Hammond played Johnson's recordings of "Walking Blues" and "Preaching Blues" onstage at Carnegie Hall in December 1938, he did not realize he was giving New Yorkers their first earful of Son House blues, however modernized they were by Johnson. House at the time was at the height of his musical abilities and influence, continuing to perform with Willie Brown. Their 1941 Library of Congress recordings preserves something of their charismatic din. One strummed the basic chords on the treble strings, the other picked out a bass melody, and above this accompaniment Son House lifted his baritone voice to sing his familiar "My Black Mama"/"Walking Blues" theme. The resulting sound on record remains mesmerizing. One follower of Son House in the mid-1930s, Muddy Waters, once attended every one of House's sets over a four-weekend stand at one juke.[150] In later years, Waters declared he was "all the way" a devotee of House.

---

[150] Guralnick 1971, 46

Muddy Waters

Waters admired Johnson's records as they were released in 1937 and 1938, but despite a chance sighting in Friar's Point, he never met him face to face.[151] He recognized that Johnson got the "Walking Blues" melody from Son House, and in like manner he adapted the tune as "Country Blues." In 1941, after performing the song for the Library of Congress microphone, Waters stated that he learned the melody from Son House, adding that Johnson performed it too.

Since the age of three, Waters had lived with his grandmother on Stovall's Plantation, helping with chopping cotton and other sharecropping tasks. But he also ran a juke, kept a jukebox, and provided live entertainment, which on one weekend was Sonny Boy Williamson II and Elmore James.[152] Yet he looked to join the black migration north. He had tried moving to St. Louis in 1940, but failed to establish himself as a musician,

and soon returned to Stovall's.[153] In 1943, he decided to go to Chicago, beginning his journey at the passenger depot at Clarksdale. He had better luck there than in St. Louis—eventually playing behind the "Sonny Boy" that Aleck Miller called himself after, John Lee Williamson. In 1947, he made the first of many studio recordings for the Chess brothers, among them two of the songs he did for the Library of Congress six years earlier, "I Feel Like Going Home" (a remake of "Country Blues") and "I Can't Be Satisfied." The initial release of these songs on the Aristocrat label sold out within twenty-four hours.[154] It could therefore be said that through House's "Walking Blues," Waters gained his first success in the north.

The Twilight of the St. Louis Pianists

The St. Louis piano blues scene continued through the end of the 1930s. Unfortunately, Peetie Wheatstraw died in 1941 in an auto accident—a misfortune that robbed blues of one of its best-selling recording artists. Other musicians like Henry Townsend, Wesley Wallace, and Henry Brown drifted into obscurity when the blues followed new trends during the 1940s and 1950s, but they were rediscovered in the 1960s. In the early 1940s, Roosevelt Sykes began spending more time in Chicago, but continued to make records for black listeners through the early 1950s; and with the development of the vinyl LP, he began a distinguished series of albums for jazz fans and white record buyers. In later years, he was based in New Orleans, but from the 1960s until his death in 1984, Sykes remained everywhere a blues/jazz club and festival favorite.

The history and importance of the 1930s St. Louis piano blues has long been passed over for the more exciting 1950s Chicago developments of Muddy Waters and Howlin' Wolf. This is in large part due to the guitar surpassing the piano as the predominant blues instrument on stage and in the home during the emerging popularity among white fans of blues, folk, and rock from the late 1950s through the 1970s. Through the years, the specific functions of certain piano blues devices were forgotten. Robert Johnson's guitar interpretations of them were heard by younger critics and listeners as depictive of what they thought of as his haunted, tortured soul. Only recently have the classic 1930s recordings of Leroy Carr, Roosevelt Sykes, and their St. Louis blues associates been collected and made available on CD by Document Records. The survey of the St. Louis style in chapters four and five offers only a tantalizing glimpse of the musical delights to be rediscovered by future researchers.

---

[151] O'Neal and Van Singel 1985, 16
[152] O'Neal and van Singel 1985, 17
[153] O'Neal and van Singel, 23-24
[154] O'Neal and van Singel, 35

The Legacy of Robert Johnson

Considering that the blues melodies and styles played by Johnson came before and continued after his performing years, it is a tenable conclusion that the history of popular music, including rock, would have been unchanged had Johnson never lived. Blues guitar players would have still tried to copy what they heard from pianists, and they would have needed the new electric instruments to produce the loud brash sounds that would inspire the rock musicians in the 1960s.

But Robert Johnson did live, and in his time he was a musical catalyst, speeding up the rate of musical development among his contemporaries. He consolidated several of the main blues styles of the day with his interrelated set of guitar tunings and his distinctive fretting technique. He shifted the focus of listening from linear melodies to vertical homophonic chords. With his piano-style accompaniment and his knowledge of city singing practices, he instilled urban musical expression into country blues pieces like "Walking Blues." Although they needed the instrumental support of others, guitarists who followed Johnson's performances were preparing themselves for transforming rural blues into viable urban repertory, and by doing so were shifting from melodic to harmonic concepts.

As an example of Johnson's impact, there is "Catfish Blues," the last great theme to be recorded by Mississippi Delta musicians before World War II. First recorded by Robert Petway for Victor Bluebird in 1941, it was quickly covered by his friend Robert McClennan as "Deep Blue Sea Blues." Its eight-measure tune may be sacred in origin, similar as it is to "I Know That His Blood Can Make Me Whole" as recorded by Blind Willie Johnson in 1927. It is tempting to think what Robert Johnson would have done with this song had he still been living. But Muddy Waters treated the "Catfish" melody two different times as "Rollin' Stone" (1950) and "Still a Fool" (1951). Since he had followed much the same path as Johnson's musical progress, Waters in both versions opted for a slow 4/4 pulse and treble motifs on the electric guitar, instead of a string band style or a strummed acoustic style. In other words, both results are closer to Johnson than to the Mississippi Sheiks. On "Still a Fool" (with harmonica virtuoso Little Walter Jacobs on second electric guitar), however, Waters makes use of the innovations he acquired since his arrival in Chicago to make the recorded performance a postwar South Side classic.

From the mid-1930s through the early 1950s, the concept of blues ensembles became transformed. The early Delta groups had performed in the "linear" polyphonic manner. But little by little—perhaps as early as the 1936 Mississippi Jook Band sides featuring the Graves brothers and pianist Cooney Vaughan—the concept of a blues band begins to gather and emerge. That band concept would demand the coordination of rhythm instruments like the drums, bass, and rhythm guitar to act in unison to the arrangement of the bandleader.

Johnson, of course, recorded solo. But many of his performances, especially those of the boogie-bass repertory, are aural blueprints for a guitar-based rhythm section to follow. One man's realization can become a collective goal for several musicians as a group to pursue. The goal wasn't easy to reach, as many flawed records made between 1945 and 1951 in the South and Chicago attest. Yet several of the first successful electric blues band records by Muddy Waters, Howlin' Wolf, and Elmore James sound like Robert Johnson played loud.

Johnson's catalyzing effect occurred again, after the 1961 release of the *King of the Delta Blues Singers* album in the United States and England. Although young white guitarists like Johnny Winter in Texas and Eric Clapton and Keith Richards in London had their picks among American blues and folk musicians to study, their listening to the Johnson album quickly narrowed their choices and shaped the styles of rock music they each developed. A similar effect may have resulted from the 1990 CD reissue of Johnson's sessions, although it is too soon to tell whether the changes have been innovative or merely imitative.

Delta swamp, north Leflore County, Mississippi

Critical viewpoints of Robert Johnson have varied. John Hammond called him the "greatest primitive blues singer."[155] David Evans[156] referred to Johnson's combination of rural and urban blues elements as "a remarkable stylistic synthesis," but does not describe the musical necessity for such a synthesis, or the consequences of it. As far back as his musical encounter with Arthur Petties, Johnson may have sought to solve the rough problems of the Delta sound with the suave solutions offered by big-city pianists. This resulted in his instilling an urban tinge to rural southern blues expressions. Had he lived long enough to witness the development of large metropolitan centers in the South, he could have helped refine an emerging southern urban style.

Other commentators have written that Johnson sounded "much more 'modern' than his contemporaries,"[157] and that he was "the Father of Rock and Roll."[158] Rock listeners seeking a musical father are like Johnson seeking his own father in Hazlehurst. They sift through hundreds of names and piles of records, eventually choosing someone whom most fits their musical preferences and views. Even if Johnson did find his biological father, he seemed instead to spend more time with his blues teacher, Ike Zinnerman. Likewise, pianist Jabo Williams could well be the true father of rock 'n' roll, but most present-day listeners have instead chosen Robert Johnson, who was a guitar player and whose songs were covered in the 1960s by white rock groups. The title "Father of Rock 'n' Roll" reflects not on Johnson in his own time, but on current attitudes resulting from 50 years of rock that was shaped in part by Muddy Waters. The more Johnson is represented as "modern" and "rock," the more his 1920s and 1930s musical aspects (still enjoyed in 1938) are regarded as outworn and obsolete.

[155] Driggs 1961
[156] in Oliver 1989, 40
[157] Titon to Groom 1970 (July/August) 17
[158] 1990 *Musician* cover

Some of Johnson's least cited sides like "They're Red Hot" and "Malted Milk" are reminders of the blues styles that were discarded by the early 1940s. Some of the lost blues genres of the prewar era include hokum, string band, jug band, and stomps. The biggest blues names of the 1930s, such as Lonnie Johnson, Leroy Carr, Bo Carter, the Mississippi Sheiks, Peetie Wheatstraw, and Tampa Red, are thought of as "old-timey," if not forgotten. Their past hits are heard today with some befuddlement as to why they sold better than Robert Johnson's records. Much of the truth is that the ways people listen to music have drastically changed over the past seventy years. Johnson's reputation is built on the fact that the elements of homophonic bass beats and bottleneck slide were retained in blues and later rock after his death. Otherwise, if the only record that survived was ARC 7-10-65, "Malted Milk" b/w "Milkcow's Calf Blues," he too would have joined his early models in blues oblivion.

Johnson's Great Contribution

To enact the change from linear polyphonic blues to vertical harmonic and homophonic blues, Johnson had to redirect his musical flow to a single pulsing bass pattern by means of chords. This meant reducing the number of melodic lines and the variety of polyrhythms, but the gain would be a greater emphasis and prominence of the bass foundation. The execution of a driving bass beat on a plectrum instrument like the guitar (instead of the piano) is Johnson's most influential accomplishment. It is heard best on the boogie-bass numbers like "Sweet Home Chicago" and "I Believe I'll Dust My Broom." This is the aspect of his music that most changed the Delta blues practice and is most retained in the blues guitar tradition.

Yet his most accomplished musical efforts are the homophonic harp-style blues such as "Terraplane Blues" and "Cross Road Blues." But with the exception of Johnny Shines, few musicians have seemed to want to exercise and extend this vertical type of blues arrangement. Even the rock group Cream, in its famous 1967 live recording of "Cross Road Blues" (as "Crossroads"), opted to reset it in a linear polyphonic fashion. Instead of bashing out I7 and vi chords, each musician pursued his own rhythmic and melodic strain within the blues harmonic confines, with drummer Ginger Baker providing the bottom register, bassist Jack Bruce the middle, and singer and guitarist Eric Clapton the top.

Johnson never recorded any polyrhythmic arrangements such as those collectively improvised by sanctified groups (as in Chapt. 1, Fig. 4). Some caution has to be taken in describing Johnson's music as polyrhythmic,[159] for many examples offered as such may be demonstrated as birhythmic or even monorhythmic. The vocal could be an intended and unequal contrast to the instrumental rhythm when the former is not following the latter, and treble ornamental pitches may not constitute a rhythmic continuity of their own. Discovering, exercising, and developing the vertical homophony latent in the blues of his times was Johnson's great contribution. But he gave it at the expense of polyrhythms.

Guitar Blues After Robert Johnson
Bukka White

For the fulfillment of rhythmic possibilities in prewar Mississippi Delta acoustic blues, the 1940 records of Bukka White must be listened to. Previously, his "train" songs of 1930 were discussed as evocative of railroad rhythms. As the 1930s proceeded, White kept abreast of the latest blues. In September 1937, he recorded "Pinebluff Arkansas," a Peetie Wheatstraw type of melody in which he injected the Walter Roland "Collector Man" fill in chorus 2, and "Shake 'Em on Down" in the Memphis Minnie "Caught Me Wrong Again" style. In fact, the similarity of "Shake 'Em on Down" and Johnson's "Stop Breakin' Down" indicates how current shared themes were among bluesmen that year. Before his record was released in December 1937, White was convicted in Monroe County, Mississippi for killing a man in self-defense and duly sent to Parchman Penitentiary. The hit success of "Shake 'Em on Down" led to its adoption by many Mississippi bluesmen and may have hastened White's early release.

Although White later matter-of-factly commented about his term at Parchman,[160] at the time he must have ruminated deeply on prison life and the things he used to take for granted. But he kept his thoughts and the lyrics based on them to himself, even when Alan Lomax stopped by with his recording equipment in May 1939. From 1933 through 1942, Lomax conducted, on behalf of the Library of Congress, several recording trips across the country, using bulky battery-operated equipment and alu-

---

[159] such as the "three polyrhythmic lines" stated by Titon (1990)
[160] Lester 1968, 62; Hurley and Evans in Burton 1981, 174

minum discs. Seeking older types of folk music and work chants, Lomax's trips transformed the common meaning of "field recordings" from commercial music recorded in makeshift studios for consumers' listening and dancing pleasure, to non-commercial sound examples for study and research. However, his sessions with commercially recorded musicians like Son House and Willie "61" Blackwell blurred the line between the presentation of individual artistic expression and the documentation of collective folk tradition. Payments to these musicians seened to have varied. Muddy Waters remembered receiving twenty dollars and two test pressings.[161] Son House recalled receiving a bottle of Coke.[162] During his session with Lomax, White touched none of the commercial material he was developing. Instead, he performed "Sic 'Em Dogs On" and "Po' Boy," two non-topical blues with heavy bottleneck-slide breaks.

In early 1940, White was released from Parchman and that March went to Chicago for a Vocalion commercial session. During this time, Vocalion was having its name changed to Okeh. As a result, his records would be released with either a Vocalion or an Okeh label. On March 7 and 8, he recorded twelve sides, remaking his train songs and introducing his prison blues. One piece, "Sleepy Man Blues," was based on Leroy Carr's "When the Sun Goes Down" and makes a contrasting comparison with Johnson's "Love in Vain."

The popular blues artist Washboard Sam assisted White throughout the sessions. In "Sleepy Man Blues," White does not use Johnson's ornamental tones and chords, but instead concentrates on strumming all the strings in up and down strokes. Sam follows the strumming rhythms very closely on his washboard, so the addition of an even-triplet declaiming of the melody renders the performance birhythmic. But during the instrumental chorus of "Parchman Farm Blues" (Fig. 40), a polyrhythm emerges, reminiscent of sanctified polyrhythms. Out of the 4/4 meter from White's unaccented quarter note strumming, his bottleneck treble melody in sustained whole and half notes connects with accented quarter notes and Washboard Sam's rhythmic layer of eighth- and sixteenth-note rolls. With this passage, and others like it, White's 1940 sessions are his crossroads, where he weighs and compares the rhythmic aspects of rural and urban manners of phrasing and accompaniment. A postwar example of polyrhythms by an urban bluesman is Bo Diddley's "Bo Diddley" (1955), with Jerome Green on maracas adapting the percussive effects of the washboard, and Frank Kirkland on drums.

Fig. 40 – Bukka White, "Parchman Farm Blues" (courtesy Hayward Music)

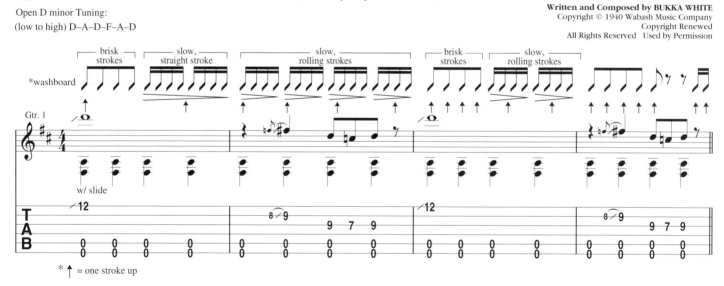

Open D minor Tuning:
(low to high) D–A–D–F–A–D

Instead of staying in Chicago, White returned to Memphis, the north point of the Mississippi Delta. During and after World War II, electrically amplified instruments became more common, and new influences were felt. White's cousin B.B. King moved in the late 1940s from the Delta to Memphis, where he began learning the blues of T-Bone Walker and Louis Jordan—two leading bandleaders of the postwar times. Turning to these different influences signaled the end of the classic Mississippi acoustic blues age. White was rediscovered in 1963 by researchers who sensed that his music had been part of a whole other time.

---

[161] O'Neal and van Singel, 22
[162] Charters 1967, 66

Epilogue

The domain of the Delta blues is best defined not by the rivers outlining the territory, or by the migration or technological trends, but through the audible sounds most artfully presented by its musicians. Robert Johnson with his acoustic guitar has long been a hardy, if enigmatic, musical model for succeeding generations of blues and rock musicians. Many of them have made pilgrimages to the Delta in efforts to ascertain his art. But the answers are not to be found in the dirt or in the abandoned shacks, but in one's ear and under one's fingers. Robert Johnson learned from those who forged the regional blues, went on to redirect its musical horizon to urban harmonic and homophonic trends that were later retained in rock, and died near the end of the acoustic era. From his cross road he has continued to stand as the most recognized master of the Delta blues.

List of Illustrations

I. Pictorial:

From Stephen LaVere

Robert Johnson studio portrait; Robert Johnson "dime-store" photo

From Gayle Dean Wardlow

Labels:

Son House
"Dry Spell Blues Parts I and II" (Paramount, 1930, both labels)

Willie Brown
"Future Blues" (Champion, 1935)

Skip James
"Devil Got My Woman" (Paramount, 1931); "Yola My Blues Away" (Paramount, 1931)

Johnnie Temple
"Lead Pencil Blues" (Vocalion, 1935)

Mississippi Jook Band: "Skippy Whippy" (Perfect, 1936)

Freddie Spruell: "Milk Cow Blues" (Okeh, 1926)

From the Blues Archive

Documents:

Robert Johnson death certificate, 1938

Vocalion Record catalogue, 1939
"Spirituals to Swing" concert ad, *New Masses*, 13 December 1938

Labels:

Robert Johnson
"32-20 Blues" (Vocalion, 1937); "Last Fair Deal Gone Down" (Vocalion, 1937); "From Four Until Late" (Perfect, 1937); "Honeymoon Blues" (Vocalion, 1938); "Stop Breakin' Down" (Vocalion, 1938); "Me and the Devil Blues" (Vocalion, 1938); "Little Queen of Spades" (Vocalion, 1938)

Louise Johnson
"All Night Long Blues" (Paramount, 1930)

Charlie Patton
"Banty Rooster Blues" (Paramount, 1929) "Pony Blues" (Paramount, 1929)

Elmore James
"Dust My Broom" (Trumpet, 1951)

Sonny Boy Williamson II
"Mr. Downchild" (Trumpet, 1951)

Jelly Roll Anderson
"Good Time Blues" (Herwin, 1927)

Leroy Carr
"When the Sun Goes Down" (Bluebird, 1935); "You Got to Reap What You Sow" (Vocalion, 1929); "Mean Mistreater Mama" (Vocalion, 1934); "Blues Before Sunrise" (Vocalion, 1934)

Mississippi Sheiks
"Sitting on Top of the World" (Okeh, 1930)

Walter Roland
"Cold Blooded Murder" (ARC, 1934)

Pine Top Smith
"Pine Top's Blues" (Vocalion, 1929)

Roosevelt Sykes
"Tired of Being Mistreated" (Okeh, 1929)

Peetie Wheatstraw
"Police Station Blues" (Conqueror, 1930)

Muddy Waters
"I Feel Like Going Home" (Aristocrat, 1948); "I Can't Be Satisfied" (Aristocrat, 1948);
"Rollin' Stone" (Chess, 1950)

Robert Lockwood
"Black Spider Blues" (Bluebird, 1941); "Dust My Broom" (Mercury, 1951)

Bukka White
"Sleepy Man Blues" (Okeh/Vocalion, 1940)

II. Musical:

Fig. 1:   Son House, "My Black Mama, Part 1" (1930), chorus (ch.) 1, measures (meas.) 1–3 (vocal melody only)

Fig. 2A: Bukka White, "New Frisco Train" (1930), bass rhythm

Fig. 2B: Charlie Patton, "Moon Going Down" (1930), ch. 1, meas. 1, lead guitar

Fig. 2C: Bukka White, "New Frisco Train" (1930), train crossing signal imitation

Fig. 2D: Robert Johnson, "Ramblin' on My Mind" (1936), take 2, ch. 3, meas. 3, train arrival effect

Fig. 3:   "I'm Going to Do All I Can," transcription and vocal arrangement from John Wesley Work, Folk Song of the American Negro (Nashville: Fisk University, 1915): 109.

Fig. 4:   Elders McIntorsh and Edwards, "Take a Stand" (1928), ch. 1, meas. 1–4, in full score

Fig. 5:   Robert Johnson, "The Last Fair Deal Gone Down" (1936), ch. 1, meas. 1–2

Fig. 6:   Robert Johnson, "Come On in My Kitchen" (1936), take 1, octave lick and thumbed-bass accompaniment

Fig. 7A: Robert Johnson, "Terraplane Blues" (1936), ch. 1, meas. 9–11

Fig. 7B: Charlie Patton, "Screamin' and Hollerin' the Blues" (1929), ch. 1, meas. 9–11

Fig. 8:   Robert Johnson, "The Last Fair Deal Gone Down" (1936), turnaround lick borrowed from Tampa Red's "Tight Like That" (1929)

Fig. 9:   Son House, "My Black Mama" (1930), ascending guitar motif

Fig. 10A: Son House, "Preaching the Blues" (1930), motivic lick for bottleneck

Fig. 10B: Robert Johnson, "Preaching Blues" (1936), descending motivic lick for bottleneck

Fig. 10C: Robert Johnson, "Preaching Blues" (1936), "quote" of House's rendition of Patton's "Pony Blues"

Fig. 11A: Mississippi Sheiks, "Sitting on Top of the World" (1930), ch. 1, meas. 1, Walter Vincson's guitar accompaniment

Fig. 11B: Robert Johnson, "Come On in My Kitchen" (1936), ch. 1, meas. 1, Johnson's piano-style accompaniment, and fiddle-style vocal and slide

Fig. 12:   Robert Johnson, "If I Had Possession Over Judgment Day" (1930) repeated fills-lick borrowed from Newburn's "Roll and Tumble Blues" (1929)

Fig. 13:   Robert Johnson, "The Last Fair Deal Gone Down" (1936), ch. 5, meas. 1–4

Bibliographic Reference List

Albertson, Chris. 1972. *Bessie.* New York: Stein and Day.

Allen, William Francis, compiler, et al. 1867. *Slave Songs of the United States.* New York: A. Simpson.

Arom, Simha. 1991. *African Polyphony and Polyrhythm.* Cambridge, England: Cambridge University Press.

Barry, John M. 1997. *Rising Tide.* New York: Simon and Schuster.

Basiuk, Bo. 1976. "The Music of Bukka White." *Blues Magazine* 2, no. 6: 41-44.

Belden. H.M. 1940. "Ballads and Songs Collected by Missouri Folk-Lore Society." *University of Missouri Studies* 15, no. 1.

Calt, Stephen. 1994. *I'd Rather Be the Devil: Skip James and the Blues.* New York: Da Capo.

Calt, Stephen, and John Miller. 1973. Notes accompanying *Lonesome Road Blues.* Yazoo L-1038. One LP.

Calt, Stephen, and Gayle Dean Wardlow. 1988. *King of the Delta Blues: The Life and Music of Charlie Patton.* Newton, NJ: Rock Chapel Press.

Calt, Stephen, and Gayle Dean Wardlow. 1989. "Robert Johnson." *78 Quarterly* no. 4: 41-50.

Charters, Samuel. 1967. *The Bluesmen.* New York: Oak.

Cobb, James C. 1992. *The Most Southern Place on Earth.* New York: Oxford University Press.

Dixon, Robert M.W., and John Godrich. 1970. *Recording the Blues.* New York: Stein and Day.

Dixon, Robert M.W., John Godrich, and Howard Rye. 1997. *Blues and Gospel Records 1890-1943.* Fourth edition. New York: Oxford University Press.

Driggs, Frank. 1961. Notes accompanying *Robert Johnson: King of the Delta Blues Singers.* Columbia CL 1654. One LP record.

Earl, John. 1973. "A Lifetime In the Blues." *Blues World* no. 46/49 (1973): 3-22.

Edwards, David. 1997. *The World Don't Owe Me Nothing.* Chicago: Chicago Review Press.

Evans, David. 1968. Notes accompanying *Jackson Blues 1928-1938.* Yazoo L-1007. One LP.

Evans, David. 1987. "Charley Patton—The Conscience of the Delta." In Robert Sacre, ed., *The Voice of the Delta.* Liege: Presses Universitaires Liege.

Freeland, Tom. 2000. "Some Witnesses to a Short Life." *Living Blues* no. 150 (March/April); 42-49

Gert zur Heide, Karl. 1970. *Deep South Piano.* London: Studio Vista.

Glover, Tony. 1965. *Blues Harp.* New York: Oak.

Groom, Bob. 1976. "Standing at the Crossroads: Robert Johnson's Recordings." *Blues Unlimited* no. 118 (March/April): 17-20; no. 119 (May/June): 11-14; no. 120 (July/August): 15-17; no. 121 (September/October): 20-21.

Guralnick, Peter. 1966. "The Rediscovered Bluesman—Skip James." Blues World no. 11: 11-17.

Guralnick, Peter. 1971. *Feel Like Going Home.* New York: Outerbridge and Dienstfrey.

Guralnick, Peter. 1982. "Searching for Robert Johnson." *Living Blues* no. 53 (Summer/Autumn): 27-41. Republished in book form with expanded back matter as *Searching for Robert Johnson* (New York: Dutton, 1989).

Hammond, John [Henry Johnson, pseud.]. 1937A. "Sight and Sound." *New Masses* (2 March): 27, 29.

Hammond, John. 1937B. "Sight and Sound." *New Masses* (8 June).

Hammond, John. 1938. "Jim Crow Blues." *New Masses* (13 December): 27-28.

Hammond, John. 1977. *On Record*. New York: Summit.

Handy, W.C. 1941. *Father of the Blues*. New York: Macmillan.

House, [Eddie] Son, to Julius Lester. 1965. "I Can Make My Own Songs." *Sing Out!* 15, no. 3 (April): 38-45.

Howse, Pat, and Jimmy Phillips. 1995. "Godfather of Delta Blues: H.C. Speir" (interview with Gayle Dean Wardlow). *Peavey Monitor* 13, no. 2: 34-44.

Hurley, F. Jack, and David Evans. 1981. "Bukka White." In Thomas G. Burton, ed., *Tennessee Traditional Singers*. Knoxville: University of Tennessee Press.

Jackson, Richard. 1976. *Popular Songs of Nineteenth Century America*. New York: Dover.

Kent, Don. 1976. "Obituaries: Marshall Owens." *Living Blues* no. 26 (March/April): 7.

Klatzko, Bernard. 1966. Booklet accompanying *In the Spirit*. New York: Origin Jazz Library 12 and 13. Two LP records.

Komara, Edward. 1996. "From the Archive" (Chart of Robert Johnson melodic precedents). *Living Blues* no. 129 (September/October): 12.

Komara, Edward. 1997a. "Blues in the Round." *Black Music Research Journal* 17, no. 1 (Spring): 3-36.

Komara, Edward. 1997b. "Son House's 'Clarksdale Moan' Considered." *Tri-State Blues* 2, no. 1 (September/October): 16-17.

LaVere, Stephen C. 1990. Booklet accompanying *Robert Johnson: The Complete Recordings*. New York: Sony/Columbia 46222. Two compact discs.

Lester, Julius. 1968. "Mr. White, Take a Break." *Sing Out!* (October/November): 4-5, 39, 45, 61-63.

Lomax, Alan. 1950. *Mr. Jelly Roll*. Berkeley: University of California Press.

Lornell, Kip. 1975. "Living Blues Interview: Hammie Nixon and Sleepy John Estes." *Living Blues* no. 19 (January/February): 13-19.

Obrecht, Jas. 1990a. "Johnny Shines: Whipped Around and Screwed Around But Still Hanging On." *Living Blues* no. 90 (March/April): 25-31.

Obrecht, Jas. 1990b. "Robert Johnson Revisited." *Guitar Player* 24, no. 9 (September): 61-72.

Oliver, Paul. 1968. *Screening the Blues: Aspects of the Blues Tradition*. London: Cassell.

Oliver, Paul. 1989. *The Blackwell Guide to Blues Records*. Cambridge, MA: Blackwell.

O'Neal, Jim, and Amy van Singel. 1985. "Muddy Waters." *Living Blues* no. 64 (March/April): 15-40.

Palmer, Robert. 1981. *Deep Blues*. New York: Viking.

Paulus, George. 1971. "Motor City Blues and Boogie." *Blues Unlimited* no. 85 (October): 4-6.

Reisner, Robert G. 1962. *Bird: The Legend of Charlie Parker*. New York: Citadel.

Rubin, Dave. 2000A. *Acoustic Country Blues Guitar: Delta Blues Before Robert Johnson*. Milwaukee: Hal Leonard.

Rubin, Dave. 2000B. *Robert Johnson: King of the Delta Blues*. (Guitar School series) Milwaukee: Hal Leonard.

Rubin, Dave, and Edward Komara. 1999. "The Origin of Twelve Bar Blues." In Rubin, *Twelve Bar Blues*. Milwaukee: Hal Leonard.

Rusch, Bob, and Mike Joyce. 1978. "Johnny Shines: Interview." *Cadence* 3, no. 10 (February): 3-15.

Sharp, Cecil. 1917. *English Folk Songs from the Southern Appalachians.* New York: G.P. Putnam's Sons.

Sharp, Cecil. 1927. *The Country Dance Book.* London: Novello.

Shines, Johnny. 1970. "The Robert Johnson I Knew." *American Folk Music Occasional* no. 2: 30-33.

Shines, Johnny. 1975. "Ramblin." *Living Blues* no. 22 (July/August): 23-32.

Snyder, Jared. 1997. "Squeezebox: The Legacy of the Afro-Mississippi Accordionists." *Black Music Research Journal* 17, no.1 (Spring): 37-58.

Townsend, Henry, and Pete Welding. 1968. "The Robert Johnson I Knew." *Downbeat* (31 October): 18, 32.

Van Rijn, Guido. 1997. *Roosevelt's Blues.* Jackson: University Press of Mississippi.

Vanco, John. 1993. Notes accompanying *Mississippi Blues* (1925-1935) vol. 2. Document DOCD 5158. One CD.

Vreede, Max E. 1971. Paramount 12000/13000 Series. *London: Storyville.* Unpaginated.

Wald, Elijah. 2004. *Escaping the Delta: Robert Johnson and the Invention of the Blues.* New York: Amistad/Harper Collins.

Wardlow, Gayle Dean. 1982. "Got Four, Five Puppies, One Little Shaggy Hound." *Blues Unlimited* no. 142 (Summer): 4-11.

Wardlow, Gayle Dean. 1994. "The Talent Scouts: H.C. Speir (1895-1972)." *78 Quarterly* no. 8: 11-34.

Wardlow, Gayle Dean. 1998. *Chasin' That Devil Music.* Edited with an introduction by Edward Komara. San Francisco: Miller Freeman Books.

Wardlow, Gayle Dean, with Stephen Calt [pseud. Jacques Roche]. 1967. "Patton's Murder—Whitewash or Hogwash?" *78 Quarterly* no. 1: 10-17.

Waterman, Dick. 1989. "Obituary: Son House." *Living Blues* no. 84 (January/February): 48-50.

Welding, Pete. 1966. "Hell Hound on His Trail." *Downbeat Music* '66 (11th Yearbook): 73-76, 103.

Welding, Pete. 1967. " 'I Sing for the People': An Interview with Bluesman Howling Wolf." *Downbeat* 34, no. 5 (14 December): 20-23.

Welding, Pete. 1968. "David 'Honey Boy' Edwards." *Blues Unlimited* no. 54 (June): 3-13.

Wilson, Al. 1966. "Son House." *Blues Unlimited Collectors Classics* no. 14: 2-7, 10-14. Previously published in eight installments in Broadside (Boston), 1965.

Woideck, Carl. 1998. *The Charlie Parker Companion.* New York: Schirmer.

Discographical Reference List

The primary sources of blues music are the records. It is a happy circumstance that over the last ten years almost all blues and black sacred music recorded before 1943 has been reissued on compact discs. The result is that the number of weeks once needed for record research now takes mere days.

The indispensable guide to blues and black sacred music of the Robert Johnson era is *Blues and Gospel Records* 1890-1943 by Robert Dixon, John Godrich, and Howard Rye, recently printed in its fourth edition by Oxford University Press. It is a comprehensive listing of every known blues and sacred record of the period, arranged by artist and session. The number of questions it has answered and of the arguments it has settled since its first appearance in 1963 is countless. For specific session data, readers are advised to consult this great work.

Yazoo Records and Document Records are the leaders of the blues reissues on CD. Catalogs may be viewed on each label's website:

Yazoo Records: <http://www.yazoorecords.com>
Document Records: <http://www.document-records.com>

Document aims at presenting the complete recordings by a given artist, no matter the sound quality of the recorded source. Yazoo, on the other hand, owns the rare copies of the recordings it reissues, and it aims to present its holdings in the best possible sound. Serious blues listeners sometimes have to buy discs by the same artist(s) from both labels. For example, I prefer the Yazoo reissues of Charlie Patton because the label gave more thought to appropriate playback pitch and remastering. However, it does not own every Patton 78 rpm disc. So for the rest of the Patton performances, I have to turn to the Document reissue.

Some remarks on Robert Johnson reissues should be made before presenting those for the other pre-war artists mentioned in this book. The standard "edition" of Johnson is *The Complete Recordings*, first issued in 1990 on Columbia Legacy C2K46222, then remastered in improved sound in 1996 on Columbia Legacy C2K 64916. The recently discovered second take of "Traveling Riverside Blues" is on the latest CD pressing of the 1961 album *Robert Johnson—King of the Delta Blues Singers,* but it isn't yet in the complete set.

Original 78 rpm copies of Johnson releases are highly sought-after items. When offered at auction or set-sale, these rarities can command prices between three to ten thousand dollars. Johnson fans looking for that special (but more affordable) collectible should try finding a first-run 1961 pressing of the *King of the Delta Blues Singers* LP with the original red-and-black "6-eye" label. Locating such a copy shouldn't be too difficult or expensive, and a well-kept copy looks really cool.

The other reissues, by performer in alphabetical order:

Jelly Roll Anderson—Document 5181.

Louis Armstrong—His 1925-1928 Okeh label records, including those with Lonnie Johnson, are on Columbia Legacy CK-44049, -44253, -44422.

Kokomo Arnold—Document 5037 through 5040.

Scrapper Blackwell—solo sides without Leroy Carr are on Document 6029 and 6030.

Willie "61" Blackwell—Document 5229. Selected Library of Congress takes on Document 5320 and Travelin' Man TM07.

Blind Blake—Document 5024, 5025, 5026, 5027.

Lucille Bogan—Document 6036 through 6038.

Ishmon Bracey—Document 5049.

Bill Broonzy—Document 5050 through 5052, and 5126 through 5133.

Henry Brown—Document 5104.

Willie Brown—Yazoo 2002, or Document 5002.

Bumble Bee Slim—Document 5261 through 5268.

Leroy Carr—Document 5134 through 5139.

Bo Carter—Document 5078 through 5082.

Ida Cox—For her "How Long Daddy How Long," see Charlie Jackson.

Teddy Darby—Document 6042.

Cow Cow Davenport—Document 5141 and 5142.

Madlyn Davis—Document 5509.

Walter Davis—JSP Records CD 605, Document 5281 through 5287.

Amos Easton—see Bumble Bee Slim.

David "Honey Boy" Edwards—Library of Congress takes on Indigo IGOCD 2003.

Fisk University Jubilee Singers—Document 5533, 5534, 5535.

Calvin Frazier—Classic Library of Congress sides on This Old World's in a Tangle, Laurie LCD 7001.

Blind Boy Fuller—Document 5091 through 5096.

Roosevelt Graves—Document 5105.

Lee Green—Document 5187 and 5188.

Bert Hatton—Document 5181.

Son House—The 1930 recordings are on Yazoo 2002 and 2202; most of them are on Document 5002. The 1941-42 Library of Congress recordings are on Delta Blues, Biograph CD 118.

Howlin' Wolf (Chester Burnett)—Career overview in Howlin' Wolf, MCA Chess Box CHD3-9332.

Alberta Hunter—Document 5422 through 5425.

Charlie Jackson—Document 5087 through 5089.

Elmore James—The Sky Is Crying, Rhino R2-71190.

Skip James—Yazoo 2009.

Blind Lemon Jefferson—Document 5017, 5018 through 5019, 5020. Selections on Yazoo 1069.

Edith North Johnson—Agram 2016.

Lonnie Johnson—Document 5063 through 5069, 5181 through 5183, and 6024 through 6026.

Louise Johnson—Document 5157, with some selected sides on Yazoo 2002.

Tommy Johnson—Document 5001.

Blind Willie Johnson—Columbia Legacy C2K-52835.

Charley Jordan—Document 5097 through 5099.

Jack Kelly—Document 6005.

Black Ivory King—Document 5278.

Robert Lockwood—1941 RCA Victor session on Wolf 004. J.O.B. label sides including his first recording of "Dust My Broom" on Johnny Shines and Robert Lockwood, Paula PCD 14. Second version of "Dust My Broom" on The Mercury Rhythm and Blues Story, Mercury 314-528-292-2. For Chess sides see Sonny Boy Williamson II.

Sara Martin—Document 5395 through 5398

Tommy McClennan—Wolf 001.

Charlie McCoy—Document 6018 through 6020.

Joe McCoy—Sides cited in text are on Memphis Minnie Document reissues.

McIntorsh and Edwards—Document 5072.

Specks McFadden—Document 6041.

Memphis Minnie—Document 5028 through 5031, and 6008 through 6012.

Mississippi Jook Band—see Roosevelt Graves.

Mississippi Sheiks—Document 5083 through 5086.

Eurreal "Little Brother" Montgomery—Document 5109.

Alice Moore—Document 5290 and 5291.

Buddy Moss—Document 5123 through 5125.

Willie Newburn—Document 5003.

Jimmy Oden—Document 5234 and 5235.

Charlie Patton—Document 5009 through 5011. Most sides are on Yazoo 2001 and 1020.

Robert Peeples—Document 5104.

Arthur Petties—Document 5158.

Robert Petway—Wolf 001.

Ma Rainey—Document 5156, 5581 through 5584.

Walter Rhodes—Document 5159.

Walter Roland—Document 5144 and 5145.

Sonny Scott—Document 5144, 5150.

Johnny Shines—J.O.B. label sides including "Ramblin'" and "Fish Tail" are on Johnny Shines and Robert Lockwood, Paula CD-14.

J.D. Short—Document 5147.

Bessie Smith—Columbia Legacy C2K-47091, -47471, -47474, -52838, and -57546.

Mamie Smith—Document 5357 through 5360.

Pine Top Smith—Document 5102.

Sparks Brothers—Document 5315.

Henry Spaulding—Document 5147.

Freddie Spruell—Document 5158.

Isabel Sykes—Document 5118.

Roosevelt Sykes—Document 5116 through 5122, 6041, and 6048 through 6050.

Tampa Red—Document 5073 through 5077, and 5206 through 5215.

Johnny Temple—Document 5238 through 5240.

Henry Townsend—Document 5147.

Cooney Vaughan—see Roosevelt Graves.

Wesley Wallace—Document 5104.

Washboard Sam—Document 5171 through 5177.

Muddy Waters—Library of Congress sides on Complete Plantation Recordings, MCA/Chess CHD-9344. The cream of the Chess records, including "Rollin' Stone" and "Still a Fool," on Muddy Waters, His Best 1947-1955, MCA/Chess CHD 9370.

Peetie Wheatstraw—Document 5241 through 5247.

Bukka White—The 1930 sacred sides are on Yazoo 2002. Library of Congress takes on Document 5320. His 1937-1940 sessions are collected on The Complete Bukka White, Columbia Legacy CK52782.

Georgia White—Document 5301 through 5304.

Josh White—Document 5194 through 5196.

Jabo Williams—Document 5102.

Big Joe Williams—Document 6003 and 6004.

Sonny Boy Williamson I (John Lee Williamson)—Document 5055 through 5059.

Sonny Boy Williamson II (Aleck Miller)—Early Trumpet sides on King Biscuit Time, Arhoolie Records. Chess performances with Robert Lockwood are on MCA/Chess CHD2-9343.

Appendix 1

Recorded melodic precedents before November 1936 to Robert Johnson's songs. Prepared by Edward Komara. An early version appeared in Living Blues no. 129 (Komara 1996).

Robert Johnson repertory	Melodic precedents
"Kind Hearted Woman Blues"	"Cruel Hearted Woman Blues" (Bumble Bee Slim, 1934)/"Mean Mistreater Mama" (Leroy Carr, 1934)
"I Believe I'll Dust My Broom"	"I Believe I'll Make a Change" (Leroy Carr,1934)/ "I Believe I'll Make a Change" (Josh White, 1934)/ "Believe I'll Go Back Home" (Jack Kelly, 1933)/ "I Believe I'll Make a Change" (Sparks Brothers, 1932)
"Sweet Home Chicago"	"Original Old Kokomo Blues" (Kokomo Arnold, 1934)/ "Kokomo Blues" (Scrapper Blackwell, 1928)/ "Kokola Blues" (Madlyn Davis, 1927)/ "One Time Blues" (Blind Blake, 1927)
"Rambling on My Mind"	"My Woman's Gone Wrong" (Leroy Carr, 1934)/ "M. & O. Blues" (Walter Davis, 1930)
"When You Got a Good Friend"	same as that for "Rambling on My Mind"
"Come On in My Kitchen"	"Six Feet in the Ground" (Jimmy Oden, 1934)/ "Sitting on Top of the World"/(Mississippi Sheiks, 1930)/ "How Long How Long Blues" (Leroy Carr, 1928)/ "How Long Daddy How Long" (Ida Cox with Papa Charlie Jackson, 1925)
"Terraplane Blues"	"Police Station Blues" (Peetie Wheatstraw, 1932)/ "So Long Blues" (Peetie Wheatstraw, 1930)
"Phonograph Blues," take 1	same as that for "Kind Hearted Woman Blues"
"Phonograph Blues," take 2	same as that for "Rambling on My Mind"
"32-20 Blues"	"22-20 Blues" (Skip James, 1931)/"32-20 Blues" (Roosevelt Sykes, 1930)
"They're Red Hot"	"Keep Your Hands off Her" (Big Bill Broonzy, 1935)/ "Keep It to Yourself" (Memphis Minnie, 1934)/ "What Is It That Tastes Like Gravy" (Tampa Red, 1929)
"Dead Shrimp Blues"	same as that for "Kind Hearted Woman Blues"
"Cross Road Blues"	"Black River Blues" (Roosevelt Sykes, 1930)/ "Straight Alky Blues" [Vocalion matrix no. C-3144] (Leroy Carr, 1929)
"Walking Blues"	"My Black Mama" (Son House, 1930)
"Last Fair Deal Gone Down"	"You're Gonna Need Somebody When You Gone to Die" (Charlie Patton, 1929/1930)
"Preaching Blues"	"Preachin' the Blues" (Son House, 1930)
"If I Had Possession Over Judgement Day"	"Roll and Tumble Blues" (Hambone Willie Newbern, 1929)

"Stones in My Passway"	same as that for "Terraplane Blues"
"I'm a Steady Rollin' Man"	"Johnnie Blues" (Peetie Wheatstraw, 1935)
"From Four Until Late"	"Georgia Bound" (Blind Blake, 1929)
"Hell Hound on My Trail"	"Yola My Blues Away" (Skip James, 1931) *See also:* "Evil Devil Blues" (Johnny Temple, 1935)/ "Evil Devil Woman Blues" (Joe McCoy, 1934)/ "Devil Got My Woman" (Skip James, 1931)
"Little Queen of Spades"	"King of Spades" (Peetie Wheatstraw, 1935)/ "Ain't It a Pity and a Shame" (Peetie Wheatstraw, 1930)
"Malted Milk"	"Life Saver Blues" (Lonnie Johnson, 1927)/ "Ball and Chain Blues" (Lonnie Johnson, 1926)
"Drunken Hearted Man"	same as that for "Malted Milk"
'Me and the Devil Blues"	"Prison Bound Blues" (Leroy Carr, 1928)
"Stop Breakin' Down"	"Caught Me Wrong Again" (Memphis Minnie, 1936)/ "Stop Hanging Around" (Buddy Moss, 1935)/ "You Got to Move" (Memphis Minnie and Joe McCoy, 1934)
"Traveling Riverside Blues"	"Banty Rooster Blues" (Charlie Patton, 1929)
"Honeymoon Blues"	same as that for "Kind Hearted Woman Blues"
"Love in Vain Blues"	"When the Sun Goes Down" (Leroy Carr, 1935)
"Milkcow's Calf Blues"	same as that for "Terraplane Blues"

Appendix II

Suggested chronological order of composition of Robert Johnson's recorded repertory.

Mississippi: the early songs:

"The Last Fair Deal Gone Down" (1928-31)
"Traveling Riverside Blues" (1928-31)
"Malted Milk" (1928-32)
"Drunken Hearted Man (1928-32)
"From Four Until Late (1928-32)
"They're Red Hot (1928-32)

Mississippi: the later songs:

"Walking Blues" (1930-32)
"Preaching Blues" (1930-32)
"Come On in My Kitchen" (1930-34)
"32-20 Blues" (1931-34)
"Hell Hound on My Trail" (1931-34)
"If I Had Possession Over Judgment Day" (1929-34)

Songs in the urban piano styles:

"Cross Road Blues" (1933-34)
"Me and the Devil Blues" (1933-34)
"I Believe I'll Dust My Broom" (1933-34)
"Ramblin' on My Mind" (1933-34)
"When You Got a Good Friend" (1933-34)
"Kind Hearted Woman Blues (1934-35)
"Phonograph Blues" (1934-36)
"Honeymoon Blues" (1934-36)
"Dead Shrimp Blues" (1934-36)
"Sweet Home Chicago" (1933-35)
"Steady Rollin' Man" (1933-35)
"Terraplane Blues" (1933-36)
"Milkcow's Calf Blues" (1933-36)
"Stones in My Passway" (1933-36)
"Little Queen of Spades" (1935-36)

The session years:

"Stop Breakin' Down" (1936-37)
"Love in Vain Blues" (1935-37)

Appendix III

Robert Johnson repertory by guitar tuning and technique

Standard (E–A–D–G–B–E), plucked:

"Kind Hearted Woman Blues"
"Sweet Home Chicago"
"When You Got a Good Friend"
"Phonograph Blues" (take 1)
"32-20 Blues"
"Dead Shrimp Blues"
"I'm a Steady Rollin' Man"
"Little Queen of Spades"
"Me and the Devil Blues"
"Honeymoon Blues"

Standard (E–A–D–G–B–E), picked:

"They're Red Hot"
"From Four Until Late"

Drop-D (D–A–D–G–B–E):

"Malted Milk"
"Drunken Hearted Man"

Aadd9 (E–B–E–A–C♯–E):

"I Believe I'll Dust My Broom"
"Phonograph Blues" (take 2)

Open E (E–B–E–G♯–B–E):

"Ramblin' on My Mind"
"Preaching Blues"

Open E Minor (E–B–E–G–B–E):

"Hell Hound on My Trail"

Open A (E–A–E–A–C♯–E):

"Come On in My Kitchen"
"Walking Blues"
"Last Fair Deal Gone Down"
"If I Had Possession Over Judgment Day"
"Stop Breakin' Down"
"Traveling Riverside Blues"

Open A (E–A–E–A–C♯–E) "harp style":

"Cross Road Blues (Crossroads)"
"Terraplane Blues"
"Stones in My Passway"
"Milkcow's Calf Blues"

Open G (D–G–D–G–B–D):

"Love in Vain Blues"

About the Author

Edward Komara is the Crane (Music) Librarian at Crane Library, the State University of New York at Potsdam. He was the director of the Blues Archive and Music Librarian at the University of Mississippi from 1993 to 2001. He earned his degrees at State University of New York at Buffalo (M.A., music history, 1992; M.L.S. Library science, 1991) and St. John's College, Annapolis (B.A., liberal arts, 1988). He edited the two-volume *Encyclopedia of the Blues* for Routledge Press (2005). Previously, he contributed chapters to the Hal Leonard books, *The Skip James Collection* and *12-Bar Blues*. He is also published in many magazines and journals, including *Guitar One, Living Blues, Black Music Research Journal,* and *Association for Recorded Sound Collections Journal.*

Photo by Louisa Gee

AUTHENTIC TRANSCRIPTIONS WITH NOTES AND TABLATURE

GUITAR RECORDED VERSIONS®

Guitar Recorded Versions® are note-for-note transcriptions of guitar music taken directly off recordings. This series, one of the most popular in print today, features some of the greatest guitar players and groups from blues and rock to country and jazz.

Guitar Recorded Versions are transcribed by the best transcribers in the business. Every book contains notes and tablature.

00690016 Will Ackerman Collection $19.95
00690501 Bryan Adams – Greatest Hits $19.95
00690002 Aerosmith – Big Ones $24.95
00692015 Aerosmith – Greatest Hits $22.95
00690603 Aerosmith – O Yeah! (Ultimate Hits) $24.95
00690147 Aerosmith – Rocks $19.95
00690139 Alice in Chains $19.95
00690178 Alice in Chains – Acoustic $19.95
00694865 Alice in Chains – Dirt $19.95
00660225 Alice in Chains – Facelift $19.95
00694925 Alice in Chains – Jar of Flies/Sap $19.95
00690387 Alice in Chains – Nothing Safe: Best of the Box $19.95
00690812 All American Rejects – Move Along $19.95
00694932 Allman Brothers Band – Definitive Collection for Guitar Volume 1 .... $24.95
00694933 Allman Brothers Band – Definitive Collection for Guitar Volume 2 .... $24.95
00694934 Allman Brothers Band – Definitive Collection for Guitar Volume 3 .... $24.95
00690755 Alter Bridge – One Day Remains $19.95
00690571 Trey Anastasio $19.95
00690158 Chet Atkins – Almost Alone $19.95
00694876 Chet Atkins – Contemporary Styles $19.95
00694878 Chet Atkins – Vintage Fingerstyle $19.95
00690865 Atreyu – A Deathgrip on Yesterday $19.95
00690609 Audioslave $19.95
00690804 Audioslave – Out of Exile $19.95
00690884 Audioslave – Revelations $19.95
00690820 Avenged Sevenfold – City of Evil $22.95
00694918 Randy Bachman Collection $22.95
00690366 Bad Company – Original Anthology – Book 1 .... $19.95
00690367 Bad Company – Original Anthology – Book 2 .... $19.95
00690503 Beach Boys – Very Best of $19.95
00694929 Beatles: 1962-1966 .... $24.95
00694930 Beatles: 1967-1970 .... $24.95
00690489 Beatles – 1 .... $24.95
00694880 Beatles – Abbey Road $19.95
00690110 Beatles – Book 1 (White Album) $19.95
00690111 Beatles – Book 2 (White Album) $19.95
00694832 Beatles – For Acoustic Guitar $22.95
00690137 Beatles – A Hard Day's Night $16.95
00690482 Beatles – Let It Be $17.95
00694891 Beatles – Revolver $19.95
00694914 Beatles – Rubber Soul $19.95
00694863 Beatles – Sgt. Pepper's Lonely Hearts Club Band $19.95
00690383 Beatles – Yellow Submarine $19.95
00690175 Beck – Odelay $17.95
00690632 Beck – Sea Change $19.95
00694884 Best of George Benson $19.95
00692385 Chuck Berry $19.95
00690835 Billy Talent $19.95
00690879 Billy Talent II $19.95
00690149 Black Sabbath $14.95
00690148 Black Sabbath – Master of Reality $14.95
00690142 Black Sabbath – Paranoid $14.95
00692200 Black Sabbath – We Sold Our Soul for Rock 'N' Roll $19.95
00690115 Blind Melon – Soup $19.95
00690674 blink-182 .... $19.95
00690389 blink-182 – Enema of the State $19.95
00690831 blink-182 – Greatest Hits $19.95
00690523 blink-182 – Take Off Your Pants and Jacket $19.95
00690028 Blue Oyster Cult – Cult Classics $19.95
00690008 Bon Jovi – Cross Road $19.95
00690491 Best of David Bowie $19.95
00690583 Box Car Racer $19.95
00690873 Breaking Benjamin – Phobia $19.95
00690764 Breaking Benjamin – We Are Not Alone $19.95
00690451 Jeff Buckley Collection $24.95
00690364 Cake – Songbook $19.95
00690564 The Calling – Camino Palmero $19.95
00690261 Carter Family Collection $19.95
00690293 Best of Steven Curtis Chapman $19.95
00690043 Best of Cheap Trick $19.95
00690171 Chicago – The Definitive Guitar Collection $22.95
00690567 Charlie Christian – The Definitive Collection $19.95
00690590 Eric Clapton – Anthology $29.95
00692391 Best of Eric Clapton – 2nd Edition $22.95
00690393 Eric Clapton – Selections from Blues $19.95
00690074 Eric Clapton – Cream of Clapton $24.95
00690265 Eric Clapton – E.C. Was Here $19.95
00690010 Eric Clapton – From the Cradle $19.95
00690716 Eric Clapton – Me and Mr. Johnson $19.95
00690263 Eric Clapton – Slowhand $19.95
00694873 Eric Clapton – Timepieces $19.95
00694869 Eric Clapton – Unplugged $22.95
00690415 Clapton Chronicles – Best of Eric Clapton $18.95
00694896 John Mayall/Eric Clapton – Bluesbreakers $19.95
00690162 Best of the Clash $19.95
00690828 Coheed & Cambria – Good Apollo I'm Burning Star, IV, Vol. 1: From Fear Through the Eyes of Madness $19.95
00690682 Coldplay – Live in 2003 .... $19.95
00690494 Coldplay – Parachutes $19.95
00690593 Coldplay – A Rush of Blood to the Head $19.95
00690806 Coldplay – X & Y $19.95
00694940 Counting Crows – August & Everything After $19.95
00690405 Counting Crows – This Desert Life $19.95
00694840 Cream – Disraeli Gears $19.95
00690838 Cream – Royal Albert Hall: London May 2-3-5-6 2005 .... $22.95
00690285 Cream – Those Were the Days $17.95
00690856 Creed – Greatest Hits $22.95
00690401 Creed – Human Clay $19.95
00690352 Creed – My Own Prison $19.95
00690551 Creed – Weathered $19.95
00690819 Best of Creedence Clearwater Revival $19.95
00690572 Steve Cropper – Soul Man $19.95
00690613 Best of Crosby, Stills & Nash $19.95
00690777 Crossfade $19.95
00699521 The Cure – Greatest Hits $24.95
00690637 Best of Dick Dale $19.95
00690184 dc Talk – Jesus Freak $19.95
00690822 Best of Alex De Grassi $19.95
00690289 Best of Deep Purple $17.95
00690784 Best of Def Leppard $19.95
00694831 Derek and the Dominos – Layla & Other Assorted Love Songs $19.95
00690384 Best of Ani DiFranco $19.95
00690322 Ani DiFranco – Little Plastic Castle $19.95
00690191 Dire Straits – Money for Nothing $24.95
00695382 Very Best of Dire Straits – Sultans of Swing $19.95
00690347 The Doors – Anthology $22.95
00690348 The Doors – Essential Guitar Collection $16.95
00690250 Best of Duane Eddy $16.95
00690533 Electric Light Orchestra Guitar Collection $19.95
00690555 Best of Melissa Etheridge $19.95
00690524 Melissa Etheridge – Skin $19.95
00690496 Best of Everclear $19.95
00690515 Extreme II – Pornograffitti $19.95
00690810 Fall Out Boy – From Under the Cork Tree $19.95
00690664 Best of Fleetwood Mac $19.95
00690870 Flyleaf $19.95
00690734 Franz Ferdinand $19.95
00694920 Best of Free $19.95
00690257 John Fogerty – Blue Moon Swamp $19.95
00690235 Foo Fighters – The Colour and the Shape $19.95
00690808 Foo Fighters – In Your Honor $19.95
00690595 Foo Fighters – One by One $19.95
00690394 Foo Fighters – There Is Nothing Left to Lose $19.95
00690805 Best of Robben Ford $19.95
00690222 G3 Live – Joe Satriani, Steve Vai, and Eric Johnson $22.95
00694807 Danny Gatton – 88 Elmira St $19.95
00690438 Genesis Guitar Anthology $19.95
00690753 Best of Godsmack $19.95
00120167 Godsmack $19.95
00690848 Godsmack – IV $19.95
00690338 Goo Goo Dolls – Dizzy Up the Girl $19.95
00690576 Goo Goo Dolls – Gutterflower $19.95
00690773 Good Charlotte – Chronicles of Life and Death $19.95
00690601 Good Charlotte – The Young and the Hopeless $19.95
00690117 John Gorka Collection $19.95
00690591 Patty Griffin – Guitar Collection $19.95
00690114 Buddy Guy Collection Vol. A-J $22.95
00690193 Buddy Guy Collection Vol. L-Y $22.95
00690697 Best of Jim Hall $19.95
00690840 Ben Harper – Both Sides of the Gun $19.95
00694798 George Harrison Anthology $19.95
00690778 Hawk Nelson – Letters to the President $19.95
00690068 Return of the Hellecasters $19.95
00692930 Jimi Hendrix – Are You Experienced? $24.95
00692931 Jimi Hendrix – Axis: Bold As Love $22.95
00690304 Jimi Hendrix – Band of Gypsys $22.95
00690321 Jimi Hendrix – BBC Sessions $22.95
00690608 Jimi Hendrix – Blue Wild Angel $24.95
00694944 Jimi Hendrix – Blues $24.95
00692932 Jimi Hendrix – Electric Ladyland $24.95
00660099 Jimi Hendrix – Radio One $24.95
00690602 Jimi Hendrix – Smash Hits $19.95
00690017 Jimi Hendrix – Woodstock $24.95
00690843 H.I.M. – Dark Light $19.95
00690869 Hinder – Extreme Behavior $19.95
00660029 Buddy Holly $19.95
00660169 John Lee Hooker – A Blues Legend $19.95
00694905 Howlin' Wolf $19.95
00690692 Very Best of Billy Idol $19.95
00690688 Incubus – A Crow Left of the Murder $19.95
00690457 Incubus – Make Yourself $19.95
00690544 Incubus – Morningview $19.95
00690136 Indigo Girls – 1200 Curfews $22.95
00690790 Iron Maiden Anthology $24.95
00690730 Alan Jackson – Guitar Collection $19.95
00694938 Elmore James – Master Electric Slide Guitar $19.95
00690652 Best of Jane's Addiction $19.95
00690721 Jet – Get Born $19.95
00690684 Jethro Tull – Aqualung $19.95
00690647 Best of Jewel $19.95
00694833 Billy Joel for Guitar $19.95
00690814 John5 – Songs for Sanity $19.95
00690751 John5 – Vertigo $19.95
00694912 Eric Johnson – Ah Via Musicom $19.95
00690660 Best of Eric Johnson $19.95
00690845 Eric Johnson – Bloom $19.95
00690169 Eric Johnson – Venus Isle $22.95
00690846 Jack Johnson and Friends – Sing-A-Longs and Lullabies for the Film Curious George $19.95
00690271 Robert Johnson – The New Transcriptions $24.95
00699131 Best of Janis Joplin $19.95
00690427 Best of Judas Priest $19.95
00690651 Juanes – Exitos de Juanes $19.95
00690277 Best of Kansas $19.95
00690742 The Killers – Hot Fuss $19.95
00690504 Very Best of Albert King $19.95
00690444 B.B. King & Eric Clapton – Riding with the King $19.95
00690134 Freddie King Collection $19.95
00690339 Best of the Kinks $19.95
00690157 Kiss – Alive! $19.95
00694903 Best of Kiss for Guitar $24.95
00690164 Mark Knopfler Guitar – Vol. 1 .... $19.95
00690163 Mark Knopfler/Chet Atkins – Neck and Neck $19.95
00690780 Korn – Greatest Hits, Volume 1 .... $22.95
00690836 Korn – See You on the Other Side $19.95
00690377 Kris Kristofferson Collection $17.95
00690861 Kutless – Hearts of the Innocent $19.95
00690834 Lamb of God – Ashes of the Wake $19.95
00690875 Lamb of God – Sacrament $19.95
00690823 Ray LaMontagne – Trouble $19.95
00690658 Johnny Lang – Long Time Coming $19.95
00690726 Avril Lavigne – Under My Skin $19.95
00690679 John Lennon – Guitar Collection $19.95
00690279 Ottmar Liebert + Luna Negra – Opium Highlights $19.95
00690785 Best of Limp Bizkit $19.95
00690781 Linkin Park – Hybrid Theory $22.95

RECORDED VERSIONS GUITAR®

AUTHENTIC TRANSCRIPTIONS WITH NOTES AND TABLATURE

00690782 Linkin Park – Meteora $22.95
00690783 Best of Live $19.95
00699623 Best of Chuck Loeb $19.95
00690743 Los Lonely Boys $19.95
00690876 Los Lonely Boys – Sacred $19.95
00690720 Lostprophets – Start Something $19.95
00690525 Best of George Lynch $19.95
00694954 New Best of Lynyrd Skynyrd $19.95
00690752 Lynyrd Skynyrd – Street Survivors $19.95
00690577 Yngwie Malmsteen – Anthology $24.95
00694845 Yngwie Malmsteen – Fire and Ice $19.95
00694755 Yngwie Malmsteen's Rising Force $19.95
00694757 Yngwie Malmsteen – Trilogy $19.95
00690754 Marilyn Manson – Lest We Forget $19.95
00694956 Bob Marley – Legend $19.95
00690548 Very Best of Bob Marley & The Wailers – One Love $19.95
00694945 Bob Marley – Songs of Freedom $24.95
00690748 Maroon5 – 1.22.03 Acoustic $19.95
00690657 Maroon5 – Songs About Jane $19.95
00690442 Matchbox 20 – Mad Season $19.95
00690616 Matchbox 20 – More Than You Think You Are $19.95
00690239 Matchbox 20 – Yourself or Someone like You $19.95
00690382 Sarah McLachlan – Mirrorball $19.95
00690354 Sarah McLachlan – Surfacing $19.95
00120080 Don McLean Songbook $19.95
00694952 Megadeth – Countdown to Extinction $19.95
00690244 Megadeth – Cryptic Writings $19.95
00694951 Megadeth – Rust in Peace $22.95
00694953 Megadeth – Selections from Peace Sells...But Who's Buying? & So Far, So Good...So What! $22.95
00690768 Megadeth – The System Has Failed $19.95
00690495 Megadeth – The World Needs a Hero $19.95
00690011 Megadeth – Youthanasia $19.95
00690505 John Mellencamp Guitar Collection $19.95
00690562 Pat Metheny – Bright Size Life $19.95
00690646 Pat Metheny – One Quiet Night $19.95
00690559 Pat Metheny – Question & Answer $19.95
00690565 Pat Metheny – Rejoicing $19.95
00690558 Pat Metheny Trio – 99>00 $19.95
00690561 Pat Metheny Trio – Live $22.95
00690040 Steve Miller Band Greatest Hits $19.95
00690769 Modest Mouse – Good News for People Who Love Bad News $19.95
00694802 Gary Moore – Still Got the Blues $19.95
00690103 Alanis Morissette – Jagged Little Pill $19.95
00690786 Mudvayne – The End of All Things to Come $22.95
00690787 Mudvayne – L.D. 50 $22.95
00690794 Mudvayne – Lost and Found $19.95
00690500 Ricky Nelson Guitar Collection $17.95
00690722 New Found Glory – Catalyst $19.95
00690345 Best of Newsboys $17.95
00690611 Nirvana $22.95
00694895 Nirvana – Bleach $19.95
00690189 Nirvana – From the Muddy Banks of the Wishkah $19.95
00694913 Nirvana – In Utero $19.95
00694901 Nirvana – Incesticide $19.95
00694883 Nirvana – Nevermind $19.95
00690026 Nirvana – Unplugged in York $19.95
00120112 No Doubt – Tragic Kingdom $22.95
00690159 Oasis – Definitely Maybe $19.95
00690121 Oasis – (What's the Story) Morning Glory $19.95
00690226 Oasis – The Other Side of Oasis $19.95
00690358 The Offspring – Americana $19.95
00690807 The Offspring – Greatest Hits $19.95
00690203 The Offspring – Smash $18.95
00694847 Best of Ozzy Osbourne $22.95
00694830 Ozzy Osbourne – No More Tears $19.95
00690399 Ozzy Osbourne – The Ozzman Cometh $19.95
00690129 Ozzy Osbourne – Ozzmosis $22.95
00690866 Panic! At the Disco – A Fever You Can't Sweat Out $19.95
00690594 Best of Les Paul $19.95
00690546 P.O.D. – Satellite $19.95
00694855 Pearl Jam – Ten $19.95
00690439 A Perfect Circle – Mer De Noms $19.95
00690661 A Perfect Circle – Thirteenth Step $19.95
00690499 Tom Petty – Definitive Guitar Collection $19.95
00690176 Phish – Billy Breathes $22.95
00690424 Phish – Farmhouse $19.95
00690240 Phish – Hoist $19.95
00690331 Phish – Story of the Ghost $19.95
00690731 Pillar – Where Do We Go from Here $19.95
00690428 Pink Floyd – Dark Side of the Moon $19.95
00690789 Best of Poison $19.95
00693864 Best of The Police $19.95
00690299 Best of Elvis: The King of Rock 'n' Roll $19.95
00692535 Elvis Presley $19.95
00690003 Classic Queen $24.95
00694975 Queen – Greatest Hits $24.95
00690670 Very Best of Queensryche $19.95
00690878 The Raconteurs – Broken Boy Soldiers $19.95
00694910 Rage Against the Machine $19.95
00690145 Rage Against the Machine – Evil Empire $19.95
00690179 Rancid – And Out Come the Wolves $22.95
00690426 Best of Ratt $19.95
00690055 Red Hot Chili Peppers – Blood Sugar Sex Magik $19.95
00690584 Red Hot Chili Peppers – By the Way $19.95
00690379 Red Hot Chili Peppers – Californication $19.95
00690673 Red Hot Chili Peppers – Greatest Hits $19.95
00690090 Red Hot Chili Peppers – One Hot Minute $22.95
00690852 Red Hot Chili Peppers – Stadium Arcadium $24.95
00690511 Django Reinhardt – The Definitive Collection $19.95
00690779 Relient K – MMHMM $19.95
00690643 Relient K – Two Lefts Don't Make a Right ... But Three Do $19.95
00694899 R.E.M. – Automatic for the People $19.95
00690260 Jimmie Rodgers Guitar Collection $19.95
00690014 Rolling Stones – Exile on Main Street $24.95
00690631 Rolling Stones – Guitar Anthology $24.95
00690186 Rolling Stones – Rock & Roll Circus $19.95
00690685 David Lee Roth – Eat 'Em and Smile $19.95
00690694 David Lee Roth – Guitar Anthology $24.95
00690031 Santana's Greatest Hits $19.95
00690796 Very Best of Michael Schenker $19.95
00690566 Best of Scorpions $19.95
00690604 Bob Seger – Guitar Anthology $19.95
00690659 Bob Seger and the Silver Bullet Band – Greatest Hits, Volume 2 $17.95
00690803 Best of Kenny Wayne Shepherd Band $19.95
00690750 Kenny Wayne Shepherd – The Place You're In $19.95
00690857 Shinedown – Us and Them $19.95
00690130 Silverchair – Frogstomp $19.95
00690357 Silverchair – Neon Ballroom $19.95
00690419 Slipknot $19.95
00690530 Slipknot – Iowa $19.95
00690733 Slipknot – Volume 3 (The Subliminal Verses) $19.95
00690330 Social Distortion – Live at the Roxy $19.95
00120004 Best of Steely Dan $24.95
00694921 Best of Steppenwolf $22.95
00690655 Best of Mike Stern $19.95
00694801 Best of Rod Stewart $22.95
00690021 Sting – Fields of Gold $19.95
00690597 Stone Sour $19.95
00690877 Stone Sour – Come What(ever) May $19.95
00690689 Story of the Year – Page Avenue $19.95
00690520 Styx Guitar Collection $19.95
00120081 Sublime $19.95
00690519 SUM 41 – All Killer No Filler $19.95
00690771 SUM 41 – Chuck $19.95
00690612 SUM 41 – Does This Look Infected? $19.95
00690767 Switchfoot – The Beautiful Letdown $19.95
00690815 Switchfoot – Nothing Is Sound $19.95
00690425 System of a Down $19.95
00690830 System of a Down – Hypnotize $19.95
00690799 System of a Down – Mezmerize $19.95
00690606 System of a Down – Steal This Album $19.95
00690531 System of a Down – Toxicity $19.95
00694824 Best of James Taylor $16.95
00694887 Best of Thin Lizzy $19.95
00690825 Third Day – Wherever You Are $19.95
00690671 Three Days Grace $19.95
00690871 Three Days Grace – One-X $19.95
00690738 3 Doors Down – Away from the Sun $22.95
00690737 3 Doors Down – The Better Life $22.95
00690776 3 Doors Down – Seventeen Days $19.95
00690580 311 – From Chaos $19.95
00690269 311 – Grass Roots $19.95
00690268 311 – Music $19.95
00690665 Thursday – War All the Time $19.95
00690030 Toad the Wet Sprocket $19.95
00690654 Best of Train $19.95
00690683 Robin Trower – Bridge of Sighs $19.95
00690740 Shania Twain – Guitar Collection $19.95
00699191 U2 – Best of: 1980-1990 $19.95
00690732 U2 – Best of: 1990-2000 $19.95
00690775 U2 – How to Dismantle an Atomic Bomb $22.95
00690039 Steve Vai – Alien Love Secrets $24.95
00690575 Steve Vai – Alive in an Ultra World $22.95
00690172 Steve Vai – Fire Garden $24.95
00690343 Steve Vai – Flex-able Leftovers $19.95
00660137 Steve Vai – Passion & Warfare $24.95
00690605 Steve Vai – Selections from the Elusive Light and Sound, Volume 1 $24.95
00694904 Steve Vai – Sex and Religion $24.95
00690392 Steve Vai – The Ultra Zone $19.95
00690023 Jimmie Vaughan – Strange Pleasures $19.95
00690455 Stevie Ray Vaughan – Blues at Sunrise $19.95
00690024 Stevie Ray Vaughan – Couldn't Stand the Weather $19.95
00690370 Stevie Ray Vaughan and Double Trouble – The Real Deal: Greatest Hits Volume 2 $22.95
00690116 Stevie Ray Vaughan – Guitar Collection $24.95
00660136 Stevie Ray Vaughan – In Step $19.95
00694879 Stevie Ray Vaughan – In the Beginning $19.95
00660058 Stevie Ray Vaughan – Lightnin' Blues '83-'87 $24.95
00690036 Stevie Ray Vaughan – Live Alive $24.95
00690417 Stevie Ray Vaughan – Live at Carnegie Hall $19.95
00690550 Stevie Ray Vaughan and Double Trouble – Live at Montreux 1982 & 1985 $24.95
00694835 Stevie Ray Vaughan – The Sky Is Crying $22.95
00690025 Stevie Ray Vaughan – Soul to Soul $19.95
00690015 Stevie Ray Vaughan – Texas Flood $19.95
00694776 Vaughan Brothers – Family Style $19.95
00690772 Velvet Revolver – Contraband $22.95
00690132 The T-Bone Walker Collection $19.95
00694789 Muddy Waters – Deep Blues $24.95
00690071 Weezer (The Blue Album) $19.95
00690516 Weezer (The Green Album) $19.95
00690800 Weezer – Make Believe $19.95
00690286 Weezer – Pinkerton $19.95
00690447 Best of the Who $24.95
00694970 The Who – Definitive Guitar Collection: A-E $24.95
00694972 The Who – Definitive Guitar Collection: Lo-R $24.95
00694973 The Who – Definitive Guitar Collection: S-Y $24.95
00690640 David Wilcox – Anthology 2000-2003 $19.95
00690672 Best of Dar Williams $19.95
00690320 Dar Williams Songbook $19.95
00690319 Stevie Wonder – Some of the Best $17.95
00690596 Best of the Yardbirds $19.95
00690844 Yellowcard – Lights and Sounds $19.95
00690710 Yellowcard – Ocean Avenue $19.95
00690507 Frank Zappa – Apostrophe $19.95
00690443 Frank Zappa – Hot Rats $19.95
00690589 ZZ Top – Guitar Anthology $22.95

GUITAR *signature licks*

Signature Licks book/CD packs provide a step-by-step breakdown of "right from the record" riffs, licks, and solos so you can jam along with your favorite bands. They contain performance notes and an overview of each artist's or group's style, with note-for-note transcriptions in notes and tab. The CDs feature full-band demos at both normal and slow speeds.

BEST OF ACOUSTIC GUITAR
00695640 ....$19.95

AEROSMITH 1973-1979
00695106 ....$22.95

AEROSMITH 1979-1998
00695219 ....$22.95

BEST OF AGGRO-METAL
00695592 ....$19.95

BEST OF CHET ATKINS
00695752 ....$22.95

THE BEACH BOYS DEFINITIVE COLLECTION
00695683 ....$22.95

BEST OF THE BEATLES FOR ACOUSTIC GUITAR
00695453 ....$22.95

THE BEATLES BASS
00695283 ....$22.95

THE BEATLES FAVORITES
00695096 ....$24.95

THE BEATLES HITS
00695049 ....$24.95

BEST OF GEORGE BENSON
00695418 ....$22.95

BEST OF BLACK SABBATH
00695249 ....$22.95

BEST OF BLINK - 182
00695704 ....$22.95

BEST OF BLUES GUITAR
00695846 ....$19.95

BLUES GUITAR CLASSICS
00695177 ....$19.95

BLUES/ROCK GUITAR MASTERS
00695348 ....$19.95

BEST OF CHARLIE CHRISTIAN
00695584 ....$22.95

BEST OF ERIC CLAPTON
00695038 ....$24.95

ERIC CLAPTON – THE BLUESMAN
00695040 ....$22.95

ERIC CLAPTON – FROM THE ALBUM UNPLUGGED
00695250 ....$24.95

BEST OF CREAM
00695251 ....$22.95

DEEP PURPLE – GREATEST HITS
00695625 ....$22.95

THE BEST OF DEF LEPPARD
00696516 ....$22.95

THE DOORS
00695373 ....$22.95

FAMOUS ROCK GUITAR SOLOS
00695590 ....$19.95

BEST OF FOO FIGHTERS
00695481 ....$22.95

GREATEST GUITAR SOLOS OF ALL TIME
00695301 ....$19.95

BEST OF GRANT GREEN
00695747 ....$22.95

GUITAR INSTRUMENTAL HITS
00695309 ....$19.95

GUITAR RIFFS OF THE '60S
00695218 ....$19.95

BEST OF GUNS N' ROSES
00695183 ....$22.95

HARD ROCK SOLOS
00695591 ....$19.95

JIMI HENDRIX
00696560 ....$24.95

HOT COUNTRY GUITAR
00695580 ....$19.95

BEST OF JAZZ GUITAR
00695586 ....$24.95

ERIC JOHNSON
00699317 ....$22.95

ROBERT JOHNSON
00695264 ....$22.95

THE ESSENTIAL ALBERT KING
00695713 ....$22.95

B.B. KING – THE DEFINITIVE COLLECTION
00695635 ....$22.95

THE KINKS
00695553 ....$22.95

BEST OF KISS
00699413 ....$22.95

MARK KNOPFLER
00695178 ....$22.95

BEST OF YNGWIE MALMSTEEN
00695669 ....$22.95

BEST OF PAT MARTINO
00695632 ....$22.95

MEGADETH
00695041 ....$22.95

WES MONTGOMERY
00695387 ....$22.95

BEST OF NIRVANA
00695483 ....$24.95

THE OFFSPRING
00695852 ....$24.95

VERY BEST OF OZZY OSBOURNE
00695431 ....$22.95

BEST OF JOE PASS
00695730 ....$22.95

PINK FLOYD – EARLY CLASSICS
00695566 ....$22.95

THE POLICE
00695724 ....$22.95

THE GUITARS OF ELVIS
00696507 ....$22.95

BEST OF QUEEN
00695097 ....$22.95

BEST OF RAGE AGAINST THE MACHINE
00695480 ....$22.95

RED HOT CHILI PEPPERS
00695173 ....$22.95

RED HOT CHILI PEPPERS – GREATEST HITS
00695828 ....$24.95

BEST OF DJANGO REINHARDT
00695660 ....$22.95

BEST OF ROCK
00695884 ....$19.95

BEST OF ROCK 'N' ROLL GUITAR
00695559 ....$19.95

BEST OF ROCKABILLY GUITAR
00695785 ....$19.95

THE ROLLING STONES
00695079 ....$22.95

BEST OF JOE SATRIANI
00695216 ....$22.95

BEST OF SILVERCHAIR
00695488 ....$22.95

THE BEST OF SOUL GUITAR
00695703 ....$19.95

BEST OF SOUTHERN ROCK
00695703 ....$19.95

ROD STEWART
00695663 ....$22.95

BEST OF SYSTEM OF A DOWN
00695788 ....$22.95

STEVE VAI
00673247 ....$22.95

STEVE VAI – ALIEN LOVE SECRETS: THE NAKED VAMPS
00695223 ....$22.95

STEVE VAI – FIRE GARDEN: THE NAKED VAMPS
00695166 ....$22.95

STEVE VAI – THE ULTRA ZONE: NAKED VAMPS
00695684 ....$22.95

STEVIE RAY VAUGHAN
00699316 ....$24.95

THE GUITAR STYLE OF STEVIE RAY VAUGHAN
00695155 ....$24.95

BEST OF THE VENTURES
00695772 ....$19.95

THE WHO
00695561 ....$22.95

BEST OF ZZ TOP
00695738 ....$22.95

Complete descriptions and songlists online!

GUITAR BIBLES

from 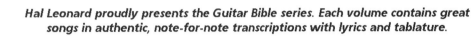 HAL•LEONARD®

Hal Leonard proudly presents the Guitar Bible series. Each volume contains great songs in authentic, note-for-note transcriptions with lyrics and tablature.

ACOUSTIC GUITAR BIBLE
35 acoustic classics: Angie • Building a Mystery • Change the World • Dust in the Wind • Hold My Hand • Iris • Maggie May • Southern Cross • Tears in Heaven • Wild World • and more.
00690432..$19.95

ACOUSTIC ROCK GUITAR BIBLE
35 classics: And I Love Her • Behind Blue Eyes • Come to My Window • Free Fallin' • Give a Little Bit • More Than Words • Night Moves • Pink Houses • Slide • 3 AM • and more.
00690625..$19.95

BABY BOOMER'S GUITAR BIBLE
35 songs: Angie • Can't Buy Me Love • Happy Together • Hey Jude • Imagine • Laughing • Longer • My Girl • New Kid in Town • Rebel, Rebel • Wild Thing • and more.
00690412..$19.95

BLUES GUITAR BIBLE
35 blues tunes: Boom Boom • Hide Away • I Can't Quit You Baby • I'm Your Hoochie Coochie Man • Killing Floor • Pride and Joy • Sweet Little Angel • The Thrill Is Gone • and more.
00690437..$19.95

BLUES-ROCK GUITAR BIBLE
35 songs: Cross Road Blues (Crossroads) • Hide Away • The House Is Rockin' • Love Struck Baby • Move It On Over • Piece of My Heart • Statesboro Blues • You Shook Me • more.
00690450..$19.95

CLASSIC ROCK GUITAR BIBLE
33 essential rock songs: Beast of Burden • Cat Scratch Fever • Double Vision • Free Ride • Hard to Handle • Life in the Fast Lane • The Stroke • Won't Get Fooled Again • and more.
00690662..$19.95

COUNTRY GUITAR BIBLE
35 country classics: Ain't Goin' Down • Blue Eyes Crying in the Rain • Boot Scootin' Boogie • Friends in Low Places • I'm So Lonesome I Could Cry • T-R-O-U-B-L-E • and more.
00690465..$19.95

DISCO GUITAR BIBLE
30 stand-out songs from the disco days: Brick House • Disco Inferno • Funkytown • Get Down Tonight • I Love the Night Life • Le Freak • Stayin' Alive • Y.M.C.A. • and more.
00690627..$17.95

EARLY ROCK GUITAR BIBLE
35 fantastic classics: Blue Suede Shoes • Do Wah Diddy Diddy • Hang On Sloopy • I'm a Believer • Louie, Louie • Oh, Pretty Woman • Surfin' U.S.A. • Twist and Shout • and more.
00690680..$17.95

FOLK-ROCK GUITAR BIBLE
35 songs: At Seventeen • Blackbird • Fire and Rain • Happy Together • Leaving on a Jet Plane • Our House • Time in a Bottle • Turn! Turn! Turn! • You've Got a Friend • more.
00690464..$19.95

GRUNGE GUITAR BIBLE
30 songs: All Apologies • Counting Blue Cars • Glycerine • Jesus Christ Pose • Lithium • Man in the Box • Nearly Lost You • Smells like Teen Spirit • This Is a Call • Violet • and more.
00690649..$17.95

HARD ROCK GUITAR BIBLE
35 songs: Ballroom Blitz • Bang a Gong • Barracuda • Living After Midnight • Rock You like a Hurricane • School's Out • Welcome to the Jungle • You Give Love a Bad Name • more.
00690453..$19.95

INSTRUMENTAL GUITAR BIBLE
37 great instrumentals: Always with Me, Always with You • Green Onions • Hide Away • Jessica • Linus and Lucy • Perfidia • Satch Boogie • Tequila • Walk Don't Run • and more.
00690514..$19.95

JAZZ GUITAR BIBLE
31 songs: Body and Soul • In a Sentimental Mood • My Funny Valentine • Nuages • Satin Doll • So What • Star Dust • Take Five • Tangerine • Yardbird Suite • and more.
00690466..$19.95

MODERN ROCK GUITAR BIBLE
26 rock favorites: Aerials (System of a Down) • Alive (P.O.D.) • Cold Hard Bitch (Jet) • Kryptonite (3 Doors Down) • Like a Stone (Audioslave) • Whatever (Godsmack) • and more.
00690724..$19.95

NÜ METAL GUITAR BIBLE
25 edgy metal hits: Aenema • Black • Edgecrusher • Last Resort • People of the Sun • Schism • Southtown • Take a Look Around • Toxicity • Youth of the Nation • and more.
00690569..$19.95

POP/ROCK GUITAR BIBLE
35 pop hits: Change the World • Heartache Tonight • Money for Nothing • Mony, Mony • Pink Houses • Smooth • Summer of '69 • 3 AM • What I Like About You • and more.
00690517..$19.95

R&B GUITAR BIBLE
35 R&B classics: Brick House • Fire • I Got You (I Feel Good) • Love Rollercoaster • Shining Star • Sir Duke • Super Freak • and more.
00690452..$19.95

ROCK GUITAR BIBLE
33 songs: All Day and All of the Night • Born to Be Wild • Day Tripper • Hey Joe • Jailhouse Rock • Money • Paranoid • Sultans of Swing • Walk This Way • You Really Got Me • more!
00690313..$19.95

ROCKABILLY GUITAR BIBLE
31 songs from artists such as Elvis, Buddy Holly and the Brian Setzer Orchestra: Blue Suede Shoes • Hello Mary Lou • Peggy Sue • Rock This Town • Travelin' Man • and more.
00690570..$19.95

SOUL GUITAR BIBLE
33 songs: Groovin' • I've Been Loving You Too Long • Let's Get It On • My Girl • Respect • Theme from Shaft • Soul Man • and more.
00690506..$19.95

SOUTHERN ROCK GUITAR BIBLE
25 southern rock classics: Can't You See • Free Bird • Hold On Loosely • La Grange • Midnight Rider • Sweet Home Alabama • and more.
00690723..$19.95

Prices, contents, and availability subject to change without notice.

FOR MORE INFORMATION, SEE YOUR LOCAL MUSIC DEALER, OR WRITE TO:

HAL•LEONARD®
CORPORATION
7777 W. BLUEMOUND RD. P.O. BOX 13819 MILWAUKEE, WI 53213

Visit Hal Leonard online at **www.halleonard.com**

0606

HAL•LEONARD GUITAR PLAY•ALONG

This series will help you play your favorite songs quickly and easily. **INCLUDES TAB** Just follow the tab and listen to the CD to hear how the guitar should sound, and then play along using the separate backing tracks. Mac or PC users can also slow down the tempo without changing pitch by using the CD in their computer. The melody and lyrics are included in the book so that you can sing or simply follow along.

VOL. 1 – ROCK	00699570 / $14.95	
VOL. 2 – ACOUSTIC	00699569 / $16.95	
VOL. 3 – HARD ROCK	00699573 / $16.95	
VOL. 4 – POP/ROCK	00699571 / $14.95	
VOL. 5 – MODERN ROCK	00699574 / $14.95	
VOL. 6 – '90s ROCK	00699572 / $14.95	
VOL. 7 – BLUES	00699575 / $16.95	
VOL. 8 – ROCK	00699585 / $14.95	
VOL. 9 – PUNK ROCK	00699576 / $14.95	
VOL. 10 – ACOUSTIC	00699586 / $16.95	
VOL. 11 – EARLY ROCK	00699579 / $14.95	
VOL. 12 – POP/ROCK	00699587 / $14.95	
VOL. 13 – FOLK ROCK	00699581 / $14.95	
VOL. 14 – BLUES ROCK	00699582 / $16.95	
VOL. 15 – R&B	00699583 / $14.95	
VOL. 16 – JAZZ	00699584 / $15.95	
VOL. 17 – COUNTRY	00699588 / $15.95	
VOL. 18 – ACOUSTIC ROCK	00699577 / $15.95	
VOL. 19 – SOUL	00699578 / $14.95	
VOL. 20 – ROCKABILLY	00699580 / $14.95	
VOL. 21 – YULETIDE	00699602 / $14.95	
VOL. 22 – CHRISTMAS	00699600 / $14.95	
VOL. 23 – SURF	00699635 / $14.95	
VOL. 24 – ERIC CLAPTON	00699649 / $16.95	
VOL. 25 – LENNON & McCARTNEY	00699642 / $14.95	
VOL. 26 – ELVIS PRESLEY	00699643 / $14.95	
VOL. 27 – DAVID LEE ROTH	00699645 / $16.95	
VOL. 28 – GREG KOCH	00699646 / $14.95	
VOL. 29 – BOB SEGER	00699647 / $14.95	
VOL. 30 – KISS	00699644 / $14.95	
VOL. 31 – CHRISTMAS HITS	00699652 / $14.95	
VOL. 32 – THE OFFSPRING	00699653 / $14.95	
VOL. 33 – ACOUSTIC CLASSICS	00699656 / $16.95	
VOL. 34 – CLASSIC ROCK	00699658 / $16.95	

Complete song lists available online.

VOL. 35 – HAIR METAL	00699660 / $16.95
VOL. 36 – SOUTHERN ROCK	00699661 / $16.95
VOL. 37 – ACOUSTIC METAL	00699662 / $16.95
VOL. 38 – BLUES	00699663 / $16.95
VOL. 39 – '80s METAL	00699664 / $16.95
VOL. 40 – INCUBUS	00699668 / $16.95
VOL. 41 – ERIC CLAPTON	00699669 / $16.95
VOL. 42 – CHART HITS	00699670 / $16.95
VOL. 43 – LYNYRD SKYNYRD	00699681 / $16.95
VOL. 44 – JAZZ	00699689 / $14.95
VOL. 45 – TV THEMES	00699718 / $14.95
VOL. 46 – MAINSTREAM ROCK	00699722 / $16.95
VOL. 47 – HENDRIX SMASH HITS	00699723 / $17.95
VOL. 48 – AEROSMITH CLASSICS	00699724 / $14.95
VOL. 49 – STEVIE RAY VAUGHAN	00699725 / $16.95
VOL. 50 – NÜ METAL	00699726 / $14.95
VOL. 51 – ALTERNATIVE '90s	00699727 / $12.95
VOL. 56 – FOO FIGHTERS	00699749 / $14.95
VOL. 57 – SYSTEM OF A DOWN	00699751 / $14.95
VOL. 58 – BLINK-182	00699772 / $14.95
VOL. 59 – GODSMACK	00699773 / $14.95
VOL. 60 – 3 DOORS DOWN	00699774 / $14.95
VOL. 61 – SLIPKNOT	00699775 / $14.95
VOL. 62 – CHRISTMAS CAROLS	00699798 / $12.95
VOL. 63 – CREEDENCE CLEARWATER REVIVAL	00699802 / $14.95
VOL. 66 – THE ROLLING STONES	00699807 / $16.95
VOL. 67 – BLACK SABBATH	00699808 / $14.95
VOL. 68 – PINK FLOYD – DARK SIDE OF THE MOON	00699809 / $14.95
VOL. 74 – PAUL BALOCHE	00699831 / $14.95

Prices, contents, and availability subject to change without notice.

FOR MORE INFORMATION, SEE YOUR LOCAL MUSIC DEALER, OR WRITE TO:

HAL•LEONARD® CORPORATION
7777 W. BLUEMOUND RD. P.O. BOX 13819 MILWAUKEE, WI 53213

Visit Hal Leonard online at www.halleonard.com